REWARDING SAFE BEHAVIORS

A Guide to Implementing a Successful
Behavior-Based Safety Incentive Program
in the Workplace

by

RICHARD WAYNE DYER

Published by
Smew Publications, LLC
San Jacinto, California (92582)

Photos/ images pages: cover© Shutterstock.com; pages 11,24,26,29,37,38,45,51,55,56,64,68,70,73,76,81,91,92,110,111,112,113, & 114 © istock photos;
pages 57,58,59,60,66,70,85,104,105,115, & 118 © Richard Dyer.

ISBN: 978-0-9982193-2-5
First Edition/First Printing

Printed in the United States of America

Cover design by Saqib Arshad
Some copy editing by Heather Densley
Prepared for Publication by Saqib Arshad

Safety Card Incentive Program™ is a trademark of Smew Publishing

To buy books in quantity for corporate use, contact the author, Richard W. Dyer at **(208) 936-1508** or email **RichardWDyer2263@gmail.com**.

This book is dedicated to my children, Annie, Becky, Rick, & Chelsea, who inspire me to be the best version of myself. If there is one bit of advice, I could give to you as you grow older, that would be, "Don't ever think that you know everything. Keep an open mind and know that useful knowledge comes from many fountains."

Dr Paul J.DeVere
PhD in Social Psychology

"Hi Richard,

In honesty, I wasn't thrilled at the idea of reviewing a health and safety book full of pictures how to pick up a box.

What a pleasure it has been to be entirely wrong about my prejudgment and as you point out in your book, we should all keep an open mind as none of us know everything.

Your knowledge of specific areas of Psychology serves both you and the readers well as we are taken on an interesting journey of enjoyable and practical application of theory into our everyday lives with a step by step of how, who, what, when, and where to apply the methods in the workplace or in fact anywhere and everywhere.

Wisdom? Wisdom is a synthesis of knowledge plus experience that only then equals wisdom and so I enjoyed the early disclosure of your varying qualifications which gave me confidence that this particular author really knows what he is talking about and has real firsthand wisdom of the topic of the book.

The layout of the book?

It's perfect, easy to navigate and written in a way owner's, managers, and workers can follow and relate to.

The use of specific examples of workers pride of their cards and including showing their wives is exemplary.

I had hoped to find something in the material that needed tweaking enhancing or expanding upon but I could not despite my own naturally negative inclination to life.

Conclusion:

In my opinion is it very well written. It's informative, simple to put into practice and benefits all those that read it not just construction workers.

Paul"

Heather Densley, CSP
ESH Data Manager, Safety

"I just finished reading the book. I'm impressed!!!!

My favorite part was the coaching section. I really enjoyed the way you taught about how to interact and how to approach each person and situation.

One more thing. I like how you talk about how to remember peoples' names, but it seems like you do it in two different places. Maybe that is a repeat?"

Heather Densley, CSP
ESH Data Manager, Safety
Layton Construction Company

Steven G. Schoolcraft, Ph.D., P.E., PMP, CSP
Vice President, Environmental, Safety, and Health

"Dyer has done a good job taking a broad and complex topic – how leaders motivate toward safety performance excellence – and converted it into a neighborly conversation with real-world examples. He suggests easy-to-do tasks that can make a difference when coupled with conscientious leaders who are already establishing and reinforcing expectations of excellence."

Steven G. Schoolcraft, Ph.D., P.E., PMP, CSP
Vice President, Environmental, Safety, and Health
Layton Construction Company

Naftoli Pickard, PhD

I read REWARDING SAFE BEHAVIORS in one swift read due to its easy format, logical applicability, and orientation toward the positive. Despite not working in the safety industry, I found its focus on positive behavior reinforcement to be a winning approach to working safely. After all is said and done, we all want our friends and family to return from work in good condition. If I owned a construction oriented company, I'd purchase a copy for all my workers.

Brad Oliver, Construction Lead Mason

Although I don't have the opportunity to work on large scale construction projects, I still think the behavior-based reward system described in this book is something I can apply with smaller crews on smaller projects. Positive reinforcement has always been something I have found to be much more productive at eliciting a desired response than negative criticism. For one thing, the results last longer. I am grateful for this opportunity to write you a positive review because I thoroughly enjoyed your book. So, take this from a tradesman's perspective, that I think your safety incentive program will reduce injuries by replacing unsafe acts with safe ones. Thank you again for the opportunity to read your book and I would love a finished copy when it gets published.

Jeremiah Ryan Cason, CHST, STSC
Project Manager, Walt Disney Imagineering

I really liked Mr. Dyer's idea about selecting 4-5 craftworkers, that performed acts safely, for a manager's lunch to show them that middle management cares and to give them a platform to talk and feel heard.

This book is an impressive perspective based on the writer's experience, evidence based facts, and real world results, The approach and implementation, creates a safety culture that craftworkers, not only embrace, implement daily, and buy into.

Encouraging and rewarding good behavior on site with positive reinforcement is something I personally think has been long overlooked. We live in a world today, where too often we focus on the negative, especially in so many other markets and business practices. When a company or an individual fails, we tend to spend a lot of time, energy, money, and effort wagging our finger, and telling them how what they did was wrong. but that is a reactive approach, and not a proactive approach.

However, we often forget to spend as much time, energy, effort and save money on the acknowledgment, or the reward of good behavioral practices. In an industry like construction, and many other industries, where worker's compensation claims and worker injuries are so prevalent, we need to ask why there is not more positive reinforcement for good behavior in the workplace.

The writer's perspective on reinforcement of good behaviors is something that should definitely be at the forefront of any safety culture enhancement program. I thoroughly enjoyed reading this book, and I plan to utilize some of the lessons I have learned on my future projects. Finally, it has reminded me to proactively encourage workers to protect, not only themselves, but everyone around them through positive reinforcement and Rewarding Safe Behaviors.

TABLE OF CONTENTS

INTRODUCTION

How can you reduce the number of injuries in your workplace? You're about to find out.

Hello and congratulations on the purchase of your new Book, eBook, audiobook, or video! (And thank you!) This book intro may be a bit different from what you may have seen in the past. This is a letter from me, the author, to you, the reader. I hope it finds you well.

First, some housekeeping. I'm going to refer to this creation throughout as "book" instead of saying all the formats I eventually intend to publish it as. So, if you're watching a video and I say "book" relax. ☺ Don't give me 2 stars! Lol.

I'm guessing you picked this up because the cover is awesome or perhaps you want to learn something new. You want to improve the safety culture in your workplace and maybe you've tried other 'safety programs' in the past and they didn't work as well as you had hoped. Well, this is not a safety program. It's not that comprehensive to be called a safety program. It's a gimmick at best that's not much more complicated than teaching a dog to sit, roll over or play dead. That's not to insinuate humans are on the same level as dogs. Or we could say it's not much more complicated than potty training your toddler. (We used M & M™ candies). Either way, training through positive reinforcement is basically the same no matter who you are training. At least in my experience.

In the next little while, we will learn how to utilize a most powerful motivational force called positive reinforcement to cultivate the type of safety culture that we should all desire in our workplaces. As a safety professional of over 15 years, I know that we all desire zero injuries on our projects and in our facilities, and that's a very high bar to reach. Not impossible, just very high. The most powerful force I know of is love and what is more akin to love than caring for your workers enough to go out of your way to acknowledge them for doing something right? I recognized as a wrestling coach of 15 years, a BSA scoutmaster of 25 years, as a parent of 4 children and now as a grandparent of 14, that people like to be noticed and acknowledged for doing the right thing. For you who have children, has your son or daughter ever said, "Mom, or Dad, watch this," before performing some silly little dance or poorly executed cartwheel? And what did you likely tell them? Probably something along the lines of: "Good job Ricky! Keep practicing!" When we send a little acknowledgement their way, something almost magical happens inside of that person and they feel validated, important, and valued. And who doesn't want to feel like they matter? I think we all want that.

Most of the time safety tends to be a 'leave-alone-gotcha' process. I learned that phrase in an amazing book called, *Green Beans and Ice Cream*." (Sims, B. jr., 2012). In it, I was reminded of something I read in another book long ago. It was so long ago that I can't recall the title of that book, I think it was on child development, but the author claimed that for every single "Yes" comment a child hears, they hear 18 "No" or negative remarks. When we observe a person working in an unsafe manner, authority figures are usually quick to jump on that situation and correct the behavior. And I'm not inferring their intentions are bad. I'm not saying that supervisor is just looking for something to get after the workers about. But I am saying that that's what we are used to doing. That's what we are used to hearing. It's normal to correct the behaviors of those whom we supervise. I mean, heck, that's our job, right? Keeping them safe. Of course, it is. Right?

Then what about when we see someone demonstrating safe behaviors? What do we usually do then? The truth is that most of us walk on by and say or do nothing. We might give them a thumbs up but rarely more than that. This is a huge mistake which can carry possible grave consequences. By not reinforcing specific behaviors, do you think we might be sending a subconscious message to the workers that we don't value safe behaviors as much as unsafe ones because we only give attention for unsafe behaviors? Could we essentially be saying, "I will take time out of my busy day to talk to you when you do something that is unsafe, but not when you do something safely?" I think that's exactly what we are saying. Children and adults alike 'act out' to get attention. It has been said that even negative publicity is better than no publicity and negative attention is better than no attention. So, let's give them the attention they thrive on and that they need. Let's give them positive reinforcement to encourage the repeating of the safe behaviors that are the leading indicators we can observe and reward to achieve the desired result of a safer workplace with fewer injuries.

But why should we treat our workers like children and walk around praising their safe behaviors? I mean, shouldn't they just want to be safe? Shouldn't they act like professionals and perform their tasks safely because it's the right thing to do and because they should know better and because they all want to go home safely? Well, yes, yes, yes, and yes again but that's not reality. The reality is that nobody's perfect. It's so cliché but it's true. The reality is that people are prone to rushing, fatigue, frustration, and complacency. The truth is that some people tend to drift off during safety orientations especially when this is perhaps the superintendent's twenty-nineth safety orientation since this project began and it isn't quite as exciting teaching the same things repeatedly. Mr. Superintendent might have a subcontractor's meeting in 25 minutes so "we have to hurry and get this done." That's reality. Maybe it's Monday morning and two of the new workers stayed up too late binge watching their favorite series on Netflix, or wherever. Perhaps someone's grandparent just passed away and they really don't feel like being here. This is reality. It could be anything really, but the truth is we don't live in a perfect world, so we need to be alert for signs that something is not quite right and be prepared to adjust.

At most companies I have worked, everyone has 'stop-work' authority. If at any time a worker thinks or feels that something is wrong, is not being set up or performed safely, he, or she can and more importantly *should* stop the process and get clarification whether this is the safest, best-practice, and most legal way to perform such a task. There is nothing wrong with that. But it's not always the culture we find in the field or on the floor, even though it was discussed in the morning's toolbox talk or safety huddle. The crew might have learned through experience that such practices slow down production and are often frowned upon by an overzealous foreman. And the foreman probably has his own reasons for pushing the crew. The project superintendent is pushing the foreman. The PM is pushing the superintendent and the owner is pushing the PM and so it goes. So, we can't always stop the pressure, but we can learn to recognize when that's happening and 'trigger on the state." We can learn to recognize when we are frustrated, fatigued, rushing or complacent. These are all Safe Start© (https://safestart.com) concepts I don't have space to get into here, but I strongly encourage you to research them on your own.

The reality of the workplace is that due to production pressures, we sometimes feel like insignificant cogs in a machine. To have an authority figure stop what he's doing and express his gratitude for the way he saw us working, well, it just plain feels good. And it's that feeling that causes a release of feel-good hormones and those endorphins encourage us to repeat the behavior.

The system described in this work will teach the reader how to utilize the force of positive reinforcement in a manner that turns safe behaviors into safe habits over a short period of time. Inside this book are precise instructions for how to approach a worker, how to coach a worker and how to do so in an unassuming way that helps to lower barriers to communication and makes the worker want to hear what you have to say. I know I sound a little vague and maybe cryptic here, but later in the book you'll get the nitty gritty of a proven process that works.

On one of our projects, we had one subcontractor that was giving us problems. By that I mean even the foreman wouldn't wear his PPE. Tying off properly was an issue as was proper ladder use and gloves and well, you name it. I was asked to go see if I could lend a hand to our new safety coordinator who was assigned to that project. After a couple of visits to the site I spoke to the project team, our safety person and to the safety representative of that subcontractor. I suggested a different approach. They had been reprimanding workers for non-compliance, but I suggested they might use the power of positive reinforcement to coax and encourage workers to obey the rules. I spent 20 minutes explaining to them the Safety Card Incentive Program which you are about to learn.

In two weeks, I returned, and this is what the sub's safety representative told me. He said, "Rick, I cannot believe the difference this has made. We used your safety cards and wow! Now everybody wants to play." I walked around that day and I noticed a marked improvement in PPE compliance, tying off, locking the scissor lift gates, etc. It was awesome. Even the foreman was decked out in full PPE. I hadn't seen that before.

At one company where I worked for 4 years in Hawaii, we had logistic hurdles to overcome. Having 70 project locations across several islands made it difficult to be everywhere for observations. Most crews I was only able to get to twice per year. I needed more observers. I needed more eyes. So, I trained each of the workers to observe each other and to nominate one another for performance of safe behaviors. The year before I came on board, they had 29 recordable injuries for 313 employees. They needed help and I was selected to provide that help. The problem was how to get the workers to recognize unsafe behaviors and how to get them to change their behavior to model what they knew in their head as a safe behavior. Take lifting, for example. Every worker could show me how to lift properly when asked but when observed from a distance, they rarely lifted objects the right way. I needed something that would reinforce what they already knew so I began to research reinforcement techniques.

Their amazing success was largely from the workforce's enthusiastic adoption of safety using this Safety Card Incentive Program you are about to learn. The results of this positive reinforcement system have been astounding. At this first company in Hawaii, where I developed the program, we saw recordable injuries drop from 29 to 17, then to 12, and finally down to 3 recordables for the last two years I was the safety manager there. I watched as their worker's compensation benefits paid out dropped from over $500,000 to less than $20,000 the last two years I was there.

At my next three positions on major construction projects, I used the same safety card system and am grateful to report that we had only one recordable injury on one of those projects. That was a 2-day lost time back strain injury. All in all, I have to say that personal experience agrees with the experts in that positive reinforcement is the most effective technique in helping someone to learn safe behaviors.

So, who am I and why should you even care what I have to say? I have had several careers and worked in a variety of dissimilar industries over the decades. I will spare you all the gory details of my journey, but noteworthy is the fact that Bill Sims' book, Green Beans and Ice Cream was influential in the creation of this incentive program as were the many psychology courses I took at university as a psychology major (until I switched my major to occupational health & safety). I was trained as an ergonomics coach which combined with my massage therapy history and wrestling coach background gave me solid footing in body mechanics, stretching, training, soft tissue injury rehabilitation, etc. I trained and worked as a safety observer for six years there. I don't mean to mislead you. That position was a "volunteer" position and not a full-time position, but I performed several observations weekly and gained valuable knowledge and experience.

I was a scoutmaster for 25 years, a substitute teacher (K-12) for 3 years and a Sunday school teacher for 15 years. I was a massage therapist for 18 years who thought he would try his hand at a nursing career, but that wasn't for me. I dropped out in my last semester with a 3.83 GPA because I didn't want to become a pill pusher. That's how I saw it at the time (still do, no offense to the wonderful nurses who advocate on behalf of their patients. It just wasn't my cup of tea. I study Bio-Terrain Medicine (or Terrain Medicine or True Medicine) now which is the antithesis to germ theory and perhaps a topic for another book.). The allopathic medical cartel is an industry I felt I could not align myself with philosophically, especially after having studied Bio-Terrain Medicine. (Especially after what we have witnessed since December of 2019 in the world. No thank you.)

Before working at the paper mill, I was an interrogator in the US Army where I learned to observe behaviors (body language and micro-expressions) and to 'interview effectively' (that's what I call it) with people at all levels of society. I was an EMT/firefighter (wild land & structural) for 8 years.

Incidentally, I was offered a decent job as a satellite dish installer that paid well so I left a promising nursing career and after several years as a broke single dad college student, that extra income was welcome. Living from a Pell-Grant, and part time construction work, barely pays the bills.

My satellite dish job took me to Hawaii where, long story short, I was injured on the job while still earning a training wage. After 11 months on Worker's Compensation, I landed a job with the Aloha Council Boy Scouts of America as a District Executive (indentured servant?) but was laid off after 11 months in 2007 (not the greatest economy) but had another job 3 days later (I love to work) and was injured badly two months into that new job. Are you following this? Imagine what it was like for me! So, I spent the next 6 years stumbling my way through the Hawaii worker's compensation and vocational rehabilitation processes. It was grueling. Mind numbing to say the least. I ended up homeless, divorced, and living in my truck, until that got repossessed. Then some kind folks from my church let me stay in their chicken barn where I fought the W/C system until I finally won my case and was reimbursed for the 10 previous months of barely surviving without any W/C benefits.

For the better part of two years, I used a walker and a cane to get around and it was not a fun time in my life. I ate the nearly expired food from the Food Bank, and I was happy to have it, and I ate wild papayas from the chicken farm. But eventually, justice saw the light of day and I was able to restore my ability to earn a decent income, this time as a safety professional. In 2013, I graduated from Columbia Southern University with a 4.0 grade point average (Suma Cum Laude- woot-woot!) and then I got my OHST, and CHST certifications from BCSP. I picked up the OSHA 501, OSHA 500, CESCO, HAZWOPER 40, EM 385-1-1, and a plethora of other certificates along the way. Oh, and I have my ASP and I'm currently studying for my CSP, which I hope to take in a couple of months from the writing of this introduction. Long story short, (again) I had plenty of real-world experience in safety related positions, which culminated in an ability to perceive what motivates people to do the right thing. If you continue to read, you'll discover in a few pages what took me decades to put together. I don't mean that I'm a slow learner. I just mean that I have compiled lessons learned from decades into this one program.

I have worked in a health and/or safety related industry in either a volunteer, full time, or a part time basis (and sometimes holding 3 jobs at once) for over 40 years. For six years I was in the worker's compensation system as an injured worker and volunteered with the Hawaii Injured Workers Association (HIWA) speaking at meetings to other injured workers. All these experiences have brought me to where I am today and to where I can hopefully help you.

So, lean forward in your seat, turn your phone to silent and don't get distracted while you strive to learn something new, or perhaps to be reminded of something that you already know. Best of success!

Respectfully,
Richard

Why should you read this book?

- Discover a simple and inexpensive method to reduce incidents in the workplace.
- Using positive reinforcement, you can be more engaging with your workforce and help them learn safe behaviors and turn those behaviors into habits.
- The Safety Card Incentive Program is a behavioral based safety concept that takes the most crucial aspects of behavioral based safety and simplifies them by turning them into one stream-lined injury reduction process.

Introduction to a Safety Card Incentive Program

- Historically, safety rewards were given after a certain number of safe days.
- Safety dinners and luncheons, Safety Buck$, and other prizes were awarded when workers could prove there were no injuries during a certain timeframe.
- OSHA rightfully declared that retaliation by an employer to an employee for the sustaining of injuries was against the revised standard (I'll explain more later) and since rewards contingent upon the absence of lagging indicators, like injuries, would logically discourage workers from reporting those injuries. It makes sense, because they would no longer be eligible for the big prizes and worse yet, they might be the reason their crew or department failed to be recognized with a celebratory luncheon or BBQ. Due to this ruling, safety reward programs went on the decline so two years later, OSHA issued a letter of interpretation to clarify.

- OSHA said that specific safety related activities and incentive programs were okay if the reward is tied to a leading rather than a lagging indicator (e.g., safe behavior rather than the lack of injuries and other incidents).
- Realizing before either of these rulings that leading indicators and positive reinforcement is a much better way to shape and mold desirable behaviors, the Safety Card Incentive Program (SCIP) was created in 2014. Back then it was called the "Pono Card Incentive Program" because in Hawaiian, pono means excellence.

A recent OSHA memorandum states that:

"Action taken under a safety incentive program or post-incident drug testing policy would only violate 29 C.F.R. SS 1904.35(b)(1)(iv) if the employer took the action to penalize an employee for reporting a work-related injury or illness rather than for the legitimate purpose of promoting workplace safety and health."

Objectives

- In this guidebook we will discuss how SCIP can be used to:
- Offer spot safety training
- Reinforce safe behaviors
- Identify and control recognized hazards
- Prevent or reduce both illness and injury
- Reduce company worker's compensation insurance claims
- Reduce injury/ illness related costs

CHAPTER 1
Motivation & Reinforcement

The purpose of having workplace safety motivation is to prevent accidents and injuries at desirable safety levels. We do this by replacing unsafe behaviors with safe ones. For the sake of this discussion, the term "incident" will include either a near miss, property damage, injury, or illness. An incident is not necessarily an injury, but all injuries are incidents.

The Safety Card Incentive Program (SCIP) uses scientific principles and procedures. Let's look at some psychology.

Motivation Through Reinforcement

- Negative reinforcement involves removing something as a way of triggering a response.
- Punishment reinforcement involves adding something aversive as a way of decreasing a particular behavior.
- Negative punishment is the way of removing something to decrease the behavior.
- However, the most effective reinforcement approach, and that which this SCIP training shall discuss, is called positive reinforcement.

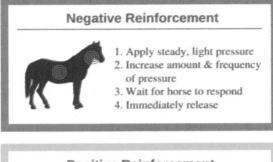

Positive Reinforcement

Positive Reinforcement is the addition of appreciative rewards meant for eliciting a particular response.

Example

- Dog handler desires to teach a dog to sit on command.
- Dog has no clue what his master wants
- While speaking the command, "Sit," the handler pushes the dog gently into a sitting position by applying pressure to the dog's chest and behind the dog's leg.
- The moment the dog gets into a sitting position, the handler gives the dog a treat and says, "Good job, Fido! Good boy!"
- Fido ultimately associates the verbal "sit" command with sitting and the reward of a food treat. When this offer is repeated, and for Fido to master it, this is referred to as a 'reinforcement schedule'.

Allow me to share one instance where I used safety incentive cards to make a change. The concept of reinforcing desirable behaviors using positive rewards was not new to me when I created SCIP. I had many years working with youngsters and adults alike. Scoutmaster, wrestling coach, Sunday school teacher, father of four, sales jobs, interrogator, and if you read the intro, you know the rest, but all these experiences have taught me that you can catch more bees with honey than you can with vinegar. Fast forward to right after graduation and after earning my occupational and safety technician (OHST) certification (and some others too) and I landed a good job with an amazing not for profit foundation in Hawaii. In my interview I was informed that in the years leading up to 2014, this company could not seem to get a handle on their recordable injuries. In fact, in 2013, for approximately 315 employees, they recorded 29 injuries on their OSHA 300 log. That's an incident rate (IR) of about 9.2 which, I've seen higher but it's not very good. Ouch! I had my work cut out for me.

Yes, I know I told you this already, but I didn't want you to have to look back to get the numbers straight. Bear with me here people. I may repeat some things but when I do it's for a reason. Remember, repetition is the mother of skill. So, the people who worked with me at that not-for-profit foundation were amazing and willing to do the work required to reduce their incident rate, so together we went to work. I will spare you all the details but not long after my hire date, the Safety Card Incentive Program was created, and we began to reward safe behaviors. The employees began to see safety as something that could be fun and not dreaded. We had 3 recordable injuries for each of the last two years I worked there. And as I recall, they were not very serious. To the company's (foundation's) credit, the workforce was able to adopt this program willingly and enthusiastically. They were able to turn their safety culture into something that any company would be pleased with. Three (3) injuries are a 0.95 IR, by the way. Pretty impressive! Insurance claims paid out in 2014 were about $500,000 and the last two years I was there the claims totaled less than $20k for each year. Pretty darn good if you ask me!

According to a Merriam-Webster search for **learning,** learning is the "knowledge or skill gained from learning." (https://www.merriam-webster.com/dictionary/learning). I have always held that learning is changed behavior and knowledge without action is wasted. (I have also maintained that you should try to define a word without using the word you are defining. But that's just me.). I will demonstrate how a small paper reward can be utilized in the safety industry to reinforce safe behaviors.

There are many ways to encourage a person to change his or her behavior. In psychology's operant conditioning, reinforcement is a term used that refers to anything that increases the chance that a response will occur. Reinforcement increases or strengthens the response. The father of this theory is behavioral psychologist B.F. Skinner. There are four basic types of reinforcement: positive reinforcement, negative reinforcement, punishment, and extinction. Of the four types, the most effective and with the longest lasting results and consequently the one we will be discussing herein, is positive reinforcement (https://allpsych.com/psychology101/reinforcement/).

Positive Reinforcement (PR+) can be thought of as the addition of some appreciated reward to elicit a desired response. One simple example is of teaching a child to hit a baseball off a tee. The coach (my son) instructs his son (my grandson) where to place his feet, how to hold the bat, how to pivot his feet, his hips, how to hold his elbows, where to look, etc. The confused child is well in over his head but he miraculously hits the ball and his Dad, er, I mean the coach gives plenty of verbal praise. "Good job son. Nice cut son. Great swing. Way to keep your eyes on the ball," or something similar. This feels good to the batter who steps back into the batter's box to do it again. The first several times the child connects with the ball the coach is impressed and let's his child know. But how often should the trainer offer the reward? In the beginning, with each ball hit. Later on, praise will be withheld unless the hit is much farther or placed more effectively. After baseball games, not backyard practice, a game ball is usually the reward of the one who hits the best, plays the best, scores the most, gets the most outs, etc. This frequency variation is referred to as a reinforcement schedule.

The Safety Card Incentive Program is a most effective tool when helping workers to learn safe behaviors. Positive reinforcement is the most effective tool to help workers learn safe behaviors. But what is learning, exactly?

- Learning a skill is changed behavior. If your behavior does not change, then you didn't learn the skill. You may be familiar with it. You may think you know it. You may even be able to teach it, but if you did not habitualize the behavior, you failed to truly learn it.
- Just because you heard it once, that doesn't mean you got it!

"Repetition is the mother of learning, the father of action, which makes it the architect of accomplishment."

—ZIG ZIGLAR

What is positive reinforcement then? Positive reinforcement is the addition of appreciative rewards meant for eliciting a particular response. Giving something, someone wants to encourage a behavior you desire.

Example:

Dog handler desires to teach a dog to sit on command, but the dog has absolutely no idea what its owner is thinking.

While speaking the command, "Sit," the handler applies gentle pressure on the dog's chest and to the back of his legs. The dog moves away from the pressure which results in him ending up in a seated position. Baffled, the dog watches the owner's voice change to an excited higher pitch as the owner reaches into a pouch for a treat and gives it to the dog. The owner says, "Good job, Fido! You're such a good boy. Now who's a good boy? Fido's a good boy."

Fido gladly takes the treat even though he still doesn't realize what he's such a good boy. Fido is smart though so after several repetitions of this routine, he finally understands that if his owner says, "sit" and Fido puts his haunches on the ground, he will receive a tasty treat. "This is easy," Fido thinks.

Because repetition is the mother of skill, Fido eventually responds immediately to the word sit by sitting. The repetition of the antecedent (command), behavior, consequence in this sequence is referred to as a reinforcement schedule. After Fido becomes more proficient, treats are given intermittently but his owner still gives verbal praise and pats on the head. That makes Fido happy.

The author, that's me, has been doing this method of rewards based on compliance for many years. I first saw the need when working for a non-profit company in Hawaii which had a less than stellar safety record. For about 313 employees they had recorded 29 injuries and illnesses on their OSHA 300 log the year prior to my coming on board.

That's an incident rate of approximately 9.27) To calculate incident rate we take the number of recordable incidents multiplied by a factor of 200,000 and divide by the total man hours worked. Now, 9.27 is not great, but trust me when I tell you that I have seen much worse. Typically, smaller companies if they have a handful of employees, they can wind up with excessively high IR's with only 2 or 3 recordable incidents. I wanted you to know how these numbers are derived.

After getting hired with this organization I knew that we had to change the way they were doing things. I implemented regular site safety inspections or audits. I analyzed the types of injuries sustained over the past three years and put them into categories. Then from the OSHA 300 logs for those 3 years I wrote down the number of days away, days restricted, and days transferred to another job, and I totaled everything up. I took the injury group that was most heavily represented and began training and retraining in those areas. Mostly it was manual materials handling and slips, trips, and falls. Those were our areas of greatest risk and the OSHA log bore that out. After the first year we cut our recordable incidents to 17 but that wasn't good enough. I had to do something more. I couldn't be in 70 locations at once, across the State of Hawaii, so I needed more eyes and more safety observers. So, the question was, how to turn these 300 plus employees into observers? I decided to create an incentive program that would focus on leading indicators only. We were not going to place any blame and we were going to reward safe behaviors. I began to study positive reinforcement and having previously taken several psychology courses back when I was majoring in psychology, I knew a little about the subject. I had also been an interrogator in the US Army, a wrestling coach for 15 years and a scoutmaster for over 20 years so I understand a little about how to get someone to do things they don't initially plan on doing. It helps if you can make them think they want to do it or make them think they came up with the idea to do it. But how to do this?

I know that people like to be noticed for things that they do. For accomplishments, for wins and even for just doing the right thing it feels good when someone you respect tells you that you are doing a great job. That he or she is proud of you and asks if you have any suggestions to improve things. That's when it hit me. A Safety Card Incentive Program! If I could catch people doing the right thing, lifting properly, for example, and tell them what a great job they just did, that should make them feel good about the exchange and make them want to repeat that behavior. As you continue to read, you'll learn what this process is and how it can completely change the safety culture in your workplace for the better.

Types of Reinforcement Schedules:

- Regular and Irregular Reinforcement Schedules
  - These schedules consist of fixed rations, fixed intervals, variable rations, and variable intervals.
- Fixed Ration
  - The application of reinforcements following a specific number of behaviors.
- Fixed Interval
  - Application of reinforcements following a specific amount of time
- Variable Ration
  - Application of responses after a variable number of responses
- Variable Interval
  - Reinforcement given after varying periods of time if action is completed.

The 'interval' of these four intervals that is found to be most effective in eliciting a desired behavior is the Variable Interval. This is the reinforcement of something following a variable period.

Example: In this event a variable amount of time passes between the periods when the supervisor checks the progress of the workers. It can motivate the workers because they never know when the supervisor shall pass, thus behooving the workers to be always ready. If the desire for the reward is great enough and/or if the fear of negative reinforcement is great enough.

The reason the positive reinforcements should be implemented randomly rather than using predictive incremental patters: Just like dogs, humans appreciate well-earned rewards that the variable interval schedule seeks to achieve.

Let me put this another way. There exist both regular and irregular reinforcement schedules. Among these types are fixed ratio, fixed interval, and variable ratio and variable interval, respectively. In the interest of brevity, either take my word for it or research it yourself but, the variable interval is the most powerful and effective. An example of this would be when a variable amount of time passes between supervisor checks of a worker's progress. This is most motivating because the employee never knows when the supervisor will pass by, so it behooves the worker to always be ready. (https://allpsych.com/psychology101/reinforcement/) It is with this understanding, therefore, that the positive reinforcement be implemented periodically and not at predictable increments.

Humans are obviously not dogs, but like dogs, humans appreciate a well-earned reward, and rewards used wisely, work well to elicit and to reinforce desired behaviors. There is one comical clip of the series

Third Rock from the Sun that appears on YouTube and treats the matter of operant conditioning rather aptly. For purposes of entertainment, you can learn from it, and I encourage you to watch it. "Positive Reinforcement – Big Bang Theory" (https://www.youtube.com/watch?v=JA96Fba-WHk)

Join me on the path to discovery as we reveal a very effective tool in managing how workers respond to risk.

On the subject of BBS, Vijaiarasan P.A (MIRSM) (Tech IOSH) at Davieli Group writes:

The importance of behavior-based safety program lies in its pragmatic approach to remove the most common source of workplace injuries or accidents – "human error".

While human error is non-deliberate, it emancipates us from our casual behavioral tendency of being complacent while undertaking high-risk jobs. Front line workers are often prone to human errors as they tend to neglect the finer aspects of safety while following routine operations. As experience manifest in faster results, these workers tend to take risky shortcuts that go undetected. This change in behavior influences a dangerous pattern that ultimately leads to an accident – causing harm to themselves and those around them.
https://www.linkedin.com/pulse/behavior-based-safety-vijaiarasan-p-a-miirsm-tech-iosh-/

CHAPTER 2

Behavioral-Based Safety Programs

The next section will first discuss general aspects of behavioral-based safety programs. This Safety Card Incentive Program is at its core a behavioral-based safety program so to understand more fully what drives it and what makes it so effective I recommend reading the following chapters. If you are a self proclaimed expert on this subject, you might be tempted to skip ahead. I wouldn't recommend it because even the stories you would bypass might mean missing out on a life lesson or two here and there.

Following that discussion, we will compare a more comprehensive BBS program to the Safety Card Incentive Program (SCIP). However, a brief review of BBS is necessary to properly implement the SCIP, in my humble opinion.

BBS acknowledges that most safety incidents involve unsafe employee behaviors, but significant portions of them have technological factors as the root cause.

Steps to implementing a behavior-based safety program:

- Secure the goodwill of management as well as of the workers.
- Collect and review the environmental, health, and safety data to determine tasks that pose the greatest risk.
- Develop a critical behavior checklist to understand behaviors that have contributed to accidents.
- Track and monitor behavior of employees during observations.
- Give feedback to employees on both their safe and unsafe behaviors during observations concerning areas they can improve.
- Leverage new data to develop improved strategies that mitigate future risks.
- Measure progress and seek continuous improvement.

Behavior-based safety programs call for the collection of information through multitudinous observations on the safe and unsafe conditions and behaviors at work. BBS involves using trained safety observers (safety coaches) to help in the recognition of any strength or weaknesses in either the employee' behaviors, or the established workplace safety programs. This BBS training can last several weeks!

The Safety Card Incentive Program, on the other hand, can be used as part of an overall behavior-based safety program or as a stand-alone program. This course teaches its use as a stand-alone program. It's quick. It's easy. It's effective. It's inexpensive and training can be accomplished in two hours (or as long as it takes you to read this book).

Antecedent-Behavior-Consequence

A model that is mostly abbreviated ABC.

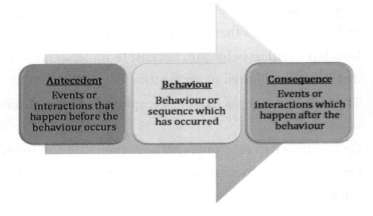

- Used in analyzing why people behave in a particular way and develop strategies of implementing behavioral changes.
- Antecedents, according to Thomas Krause, are pre-existing intellectual inputs that are used as catalysts for behavior, and which influence the consequences of a particular behavior. (Why the behavior?)
- Behavior, based on Scott Geller's description, is a physical action of workers that others can observe. (Which behavior is done or not done?)
- Aubrey Daniels describes Consequences as what happens to an actor as a result of the behavior. Can be positive or negative. (What is the result of the behavior?)
- To develop an effective safety program, analyze the antecedents that precede a particular behavior and create strategies to minimize the negative consequences emanating from the identified antecedents.

BBSP Improvement using ABC Model

- Start by identifying crucial problem behaviors triggered by antecedents.
- Establish the leading indicators that contribute to the negative outcome.
- Develop possible corrective actions that can contain the behavior.
- Short-list the most effective solution plans.
- Develop an action plan meant for positively influencing the antecedent triggers.
- Execute the plan in view of the existing and shifted ABC circumstances.
- Measure the success rate of the implementation plan.

In a nutshell, behavior-based safety (BBS) involves the use of safety observations to recognize strengths and weaknesses in both workers and workplace safety programs. BBS recognizes that most incidents involve worker behavior but that a significant portion have as their root cause engineering or technical factors. BBS typically requires a collection of data on both safe and unsafe behaviors in addition to conditions in the workplace. Usually both *planned* and *unplanned* observations are incorporated into a BBS program. This has to do with something called the Hawthorn Effect which says that people behave in a different manner when they know they are being watched. I see this all the time. Some crews even have special code names they will holler out when the safety person comes around. Watch closely as guys turn around and magically reappear with their safety glasses on. So sneaky. Not!

Consequently, I have learned to do my observations from a distance. Whereas 30 years ago I was a bit leery of 'spying' on workers, now it does not phase me at all (Mwaahaha). I even keep a set of binoculars in my vehicle so I can see if a worker is wearing the proper lanyard when he is several stories up and 500 meters away. If he is not, or worse yet, if he is not tied off at all, I drop everything and call the project superintendent to have him contact the guy's supervisor. If I can't get a hold of anyone, I go straight to the worker and address the situation directly. We will talk more about this later.

SCIP—Target Audience

10 – 80 – 10

This Photo by Unknown Author is licensed under CC BY

Benefits of a Behavior Based Safety Program

Have you heard of the 10-80-10 theory? This theory is sometimes used to explain human behavior and reactions. What is the demographic this program will most greatly affect? Based on the 10-80-10 theory of human behavior and reactions, this Safety Card Incentive Program targets the 80% group to encourage them towards safe behavior.

It states that:

- 10% follow the plan and do the right thing because they feel they should.
- 10% won't do the right thing, regardless of the tactics employed.
- 80% of the people can be convinced either way, but they seek some reward. This last group is the one the incentive program should target. By showing them how they will benefit, they'll be more inclined to get onboard.

According to Marshall (2003) behavior scientists have stated that behavior that is reinforced (incentivized) will occur more frequently than behavior that is not reinforced. This concept is the key to the entire Safety Card Incentive Program! Let that soak in for a minute people. In fact, let's read this part out loud, together.

Behavior that is reinforced (incentivized) will occur more frequently than behavior that is not reinforced.

I put it all by itself. It is literally that important. Moreover, researchers have found that for every 330 unsafe acts, twenty-nine minor injuries will occur and only one of the 330 will result in a lost time incident. What gets reinforced, when safe behaviors are not rewarded, and is therefore more likely to occur, is the shortcut the person who is behaving unsafely took to save time. The reason this reinforcement works to encourage more unsafe behavior is that the worker seldom gets injured performing this unsafe behavior. There may be a near miss (or five) but he didn't get hurt so, "It's all good." Subconsciously, he is receiving reinforcement in two ways; by not getting injured and by being able to perform a task more quickly. Three ways if you count the fact that nobody said anything to deter his unsafe behavior. Historically, it is this group of high-risk workers who sustain more injuries. The only thing that will effectively counter this risky behavior is to reinforce the safe behavior that would prevent the unsafe behavior from occurring. Read that paragraph again if you didn't get it. No, I'm serious. Go back and read it again. What's the mother of skill? Repetition you say? Good job reader! You remembered. I'm impressed.

See what I did there? ;-)

Incentive programs work. According to Smith (2004), such programs targeted at individuals resulted in a 27 percent performance increase, teams that were targeted had a 45 percent performance increase and some 92 percent of surveyed workers said that incentives were the reason they achieved their goals.

So, why might you consider a BBS compliment to your existing safety program? Advocates of safety incentive programs feel the "carrot" is a strong motivation towards appropriate safe behavior (Prichard, 2001). Workers appreciate recognition and it is an indicator that management is paying attention to them, and cares about them and their performance. Culture does not change overnight, however the implementation of a safety incentive program like this one, if done correctly, can be a cause for positive change resulting in improved morale, and a heightened safety awareness, in addition to a very real reduction of worker's compensation claims and employer costs.

If you like archery or if you are a visual learner, then this is for you:

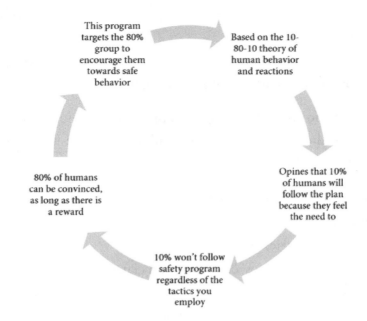

This program targets the 80% group to encourage them towards safe behavior

Based on the 10-80-10 theory of human behavior and reactions

Opines that 10% of humans will follow the plan because they feel the need to

10% won't follow safety program regardless of the tactics you employ

80% of humans can be convinced, as long as there is a reward

What Spawns Unsafe Behavior?

Let's take a quick look at what spawns unsafe behaviors. Because frankly, a discussion of how to encourage and reinforce safe behavior would be incomplete without answering this question. We all know what we are supposed to do, but why don't we do it? What are the reasons some workers fail to keep the established rules and regulations?

- Failure of management to design and enforce safety protocols (this is number one for a reason)
- Lack of adequate training
- Taking shortcuts (lazy, rushing, complacent)
- Safety culture is not conducive to compliance.
- Worker having a bad day/week.

- Worker doesn't care about safety, or it isn't high on his list of priorities.
- States of mind: Rushing, frustration, fatigue, complacency
- **Can you think of any other reasons?**

The Safe Behavior Incentive Program applies a solid motivation strategy towards the adoption of safe and appropriate behaviors. If performed as designed, it:

- Improves morale of workers
- Heightens safety awareness.
- Reduces injuries/ illnesses.
- Reduces employees' compensation claims in both number and expense.
- Ensures that employees keep workplace safety at the top of their minds.

CHAPTER 3
Behavior identification

Safe 1 Behaviors

Unsafe behaviors demand immediate response to the behavior and depending upon how severe the violation is will determine the level of discipline involved. For the sake of clarity, safety related behaviors will be categorized into two broad types. Safe and Unsafe behaviors. Safe behaviors will be incentivized and categorized into two types. Firstly, there are Safe-1 or minimum compliance behaviors and secondly there are Safe-2 or above and beyond behaviors.

All unsafe behaviors require immediate attention and depending on their severity, either a verbal warning or some form of disciplinary action, including possible termination, is appropriate. These will be categorized into three types which we will call Unsafe-1 or somewhat dangerous, Unsafe-2 or very serious and could lead to serious injury or life endangerment and, Unsafe-3 blatant disregard for safety possibly warranting removal from project., depending on your company's policy.

Safe 1 level behaviors are the basic safety behaviors or the minimum compliance requirements expected and required. In construction they include leather boots above the ankles, shirts with at least 3-inch-long sleeves, long pants that do not restrict walking or cause tripping, safety glasses, safety high visibility clothing, hard hat, and gloves.

Safe 1 behavior could be newer policies or minimum compliance behaviors and include things like abiding a recently introduced 100% glove-use policy. Some companies require cut level 2 or 3 gloves as a minimum standard or safety toe boots as a minimum standard as well. They are the minimum safety compliance standards set by OSHA or the states equivalent to OSHA. These behaviors should not be rewarded according to some schools of thought. Stated in a different way, these types of behaviors are the minimum requirement to walk onto a jobsite, and some schools of thought teach that these behaviors should not be rewarded at all because they are a mandatory minimum standard to start work. People in this camp believe that since this type of behavior is an expectation of employment, it is not something that would typically merit additional compensation or incentivization. On one level, I agree. But we don't live in an ideal world. We must face reality and the reality is that we are all at different levels of learning safe behaviors.

Why not reward Safe 1 behavior?

So then, this leads to the discussion of why we are rewarding workers for doing what they are required to do. That's a good question. I think it comes down to four things.

1) Not everyone is at the same level of awareness.

Have you ever worked with someone who seems like they need to be told every little thing? Some workers can look around, see what needs to be done, and get in and do it. But others just do not seem to possess such a comprehensive level of awareness. Coupled with this concept is the idea that the safety of workers is the employer's responsibility.

(Time out. Okay, so what I was just talking about there is actually called "Situational Awareness" and there are entire courses devoted to the subject. I highly highly recommend you delve into this concept and educate your powerful brain on what situational awareness is and how it can save your life and/or the lives of your loved ones. Now back to the topic at hand.)

Have you heard of OSHA's General Duty Clause? If you are reading this book, I'm sure you probably have. But for the scant few who may not know, OSHA has a standard referred to as the General Duty Clause. In the OSH Act of 1970, Section 5(a)(1) it says:

> (a) Each employer—
>> (1) Shall furnish to each of his employees, employment and a place of employment which are free from recognized hazards that are causing or are likely to cause death or serious physical harm to his employees;

Cutting to the heart of this standard; part of it means that companies have the legal responsibility of ensuring that all workers have a safe place to work. (Yes, I know there is plenty more in those few words but for our conversation here today, this is the crux). With the powers bestowed on safety supervisors comes the responsibility of ensuring safety in the organization. Tying the fact that not all workers are at the same level of situational awareness to the fact that employers are required to provide a safe work environment, this translates to the need for employers to make their work areas and procedures safe enough for all workers. Having said that, this is where effective hiring and adequate training come into play, along with other factors.

Whether the behavior is Safe 1 or Safe 2 the safety supervisor is ultimately responsible for enforcement of safety standards, policies, rules, and regulations. But safety is everybody's responsibility and besides, you never know how far and how wide your influence will spread.

2) We have a moral responsibility to ensure that our workers return home safely. It is the right thing to do. This is what integrity involves. Choose the right (CTR).

3) We share both the responsibility and accountability to ensure our workers anticipate a safe work environment. They should know they won't be asked (or allowed) to do anything life threatening when they come to work.

4) With great power comes great responsibility, (Peter Parker's Uncle Ben) or as Luke 12:48 states, "From everyone who has been given much, much will be demanded; and from the one who has been entrusted with much, much more will be asked." Safety professionals and Superintendents generally have more information and knowledge regarding safe behaviors than most workers.

Let us assume that you agree with the previous paragraph and that's why you are here. Then I won't need to spend time convincing you that a safety incentive program based on positive reinforcement of safe behaviors is a good idea.

This perspective, of coddling one's workers, however, depends on a company's philosophy on discipline. A company may choose to be more forgiving when enforcing compliance of the minimum compliance behaviors. Its management style may be one of giving multiple chances to workers who continue to disregard the safety glasses policy, for example. Leniency, although appreciated by the workers, tends to lead to workers pushing the boundaries. Not always, but usually this situation will be taken advantage of by some workers. Water, electricity, and humans have at least one thing in common. We all prefer to follow the path of least resistance. Humans are also comprised of 99% water molecules which are electrically charged. Give that a ponder. Giving a worker multiple chances to get on board with a simple policy, may seem like the nice thing to do, but if one of those times that worker, who continues to ignore the safety glasses policy, loses an eye, we must ask ourselves as management if it was worth it. Positive reinforcement doesn't mean we cannot be strict. Don't be afraid to be 'that guy' and send someone home if he needs a reminder that safety is important, and it applies to everyone.

Sending someone home for the rest of the day, the week, or permanently removing them from the project is seldom if ever convenient. It might leave the subcontractor short-handed. The decision could slow down production depending on that individual's role. It is a potentially confrontational situation for the safety person and the superintendent and of course it is not pleasant for the worker, but the alternative could be far worse. I have found that we can still come at this from a point of showing we care about that worker, and we do not want him to get hurt so we are giving him time to go home and reconsider his commitment to safety. If the worker has a terrible attitude, gives considerable pushback, or this is a recurring issue, then I typically recommend permanent removal from the project.

Incidentally, I don't tend to reward Safe-1 behaviors either, unless a subcontractor, which is not used to working under a stricter company's policies, warrants special coaching and nurturing. If that is the case, I will reward any behavior that I think needs to be reinforced. I have seen this system work too many times to not believe in it.

Safety moment

Once on a hotel project (City of Hope Hotel) there was this one younger worker with long hair and a good work ethic. This guy was always busy doing something, but he did not like to wear his safety glasses. At the company where I work, we have a 100% safety glasses policy so I could not let him slide. He was always respectful and willing to comply while I was in his presence but a few hours later he was walking around without his glasses again. After the third or fourth time I pulled him aside and spoke with him.

I had already asked him why he wasn't wearing them, and at least he was honest. He said he does not like wearing them. They are uncomfortable. My response was that maybe he could try different styles and I gave him some of ours. He wore them for a little while. When I did catch him with them on, I was sure to make a big deal of it. I would say things like, "Hey Sam! Look at you in those good -looking safety glasses! I bet your girlfriend is going to be happy when you come home with both eyes still intact." I also gave him a safety card when I found him wearing them when I did not have to remind him to do so. After about a month "Sam" never missed a day of wearing his safety glasses. I don't know if he ever won the safety card raffle on Friday, but it wasn't because he didn't have raffle tickets! (We will learn more about that later).

It has been this author's experience that setting the higher expectation up front and maintaining that expectation throughout the project will set the tone for the desired safety culture, where more experienced workers police the inexperienced ones and the superintendent and safety manager's jobs are easier when it comes to personal protective equipment (PPE) enforcement and other safety policy compliance.

Safety Moment:

Not to beat a dead horse, but many folks tend to think of the safety glasses rule (or even gloves) as a necessary evil until it's too late. In a training class recently, a superintendent shared with us a safety moment. Let's call that superintendent, Joe. Joe said that a subcontractor worker, who we will call Frank, and who had previously been on one of the construction projects Joe managed, sought Joe out to share a personal experience.

Frank was grateful that his supervisor had been reminding him to wear his safety glasses at work. "Frank don't forget your safety glasses," he would say. One day Frank was at home preparing to do some work in his wood shop. He had just turned on his table saw to cut a board for a drawer repair he had been procrastinating for weeks. As he began to push the board toward the spinning carbide tipped blade, he heard a voice, "Frank, don't forget your safety glasses."

This Photo by Unknown Author is licensed under CC BY

Frank immediately shut off his table saw. He walked over to his cluttered bench and smiled as he cleaned then donned his safety glasses. Returning to his saw, he grabbed his board and flipped the red switch. The shiny steel blade roared to life. As he pushed the wood into the teeth, a wood chip flew up and hit him in the glasses. Frank instinctively squinted his eyes. He removed the board and turned off the saw. "Wow!" He thought. Instantly he knew that he owed the preservation of his eyesight to Joe, and he wanted to say thank you. And yes, as you undoubtedly suspect, he maybe should have been wearing a high impact face shield. Incidentally, I ran across an ANSI Z87+ rated face shield called the UVEX Bionic Face Shield (S8500) for $33. (See bibliography)

This Photo by Unknown Author is licensed under CC BY

We know about Frank's story because Frank went to work Monday morning and shared this story with his supervisor, who later shared it with the author. (I really don't like saying 'the author' so if it's okay with you, I'm going to quit. It sounds pretentious to me. "The author" as if I should be saying it with a posh English accent). Now where was I?

Oh yes, Frank and this story of a Safe 1 behavior. Wearing safety glasses is a Safe 1 safety measure that Frank, or anybody else, should not need to be reminded about, but being human, Frank and all of us, are prone to forget, to rush, to experience fatigue, complacency, and frustration which can lead to the behaviors these states of mind tend to produce. (Study SafeStart™ for a more complete picture).

I heard a story of another worker who reported that while doing a home construction project, he was using a new aluminum oxide blade to cut metal framing. He said that in his head he heard his supervisor's voice repeatedly tell him to put on his safety glasses. The worker donned his safety glasses then began his cut. Without warning the blade exploded into shards that went flying in all directions. One larger piece struck the worker in the face. He suffered a deep cut from his cheek bone vertically through the center of his eyebrow, but his safety glasses prevented the shard from touching his eye. This is another example of someone who should have been wearing safety glasses and a face shield.

Therefore, Safe 1 behaviors should be incentivized until they become as habitualized as eating lunch.

Safe 2 Behaviors

These behaviors are also called "Above and Beyond."

Example:

Wearing additional PPE (appropriate respiratory, clothing, face shields, hearing protection, metatarsal shoes, etc.). Having additional PPE does not qualify for "Above and Beyond" in OSHA terms. In fact, "Above and Beyond" is not really an OSHA concept. A worker is either in compliance or he is not. And that's the case here too, regarding compliance, but we aren't focused on compliance, per se. We are learning to distinguish between basic safe behaviors and those that may not be quite as easy to habitualize because they aren't used every day. This level of PPE may take a smidgeon more training or experience. The supervisor and/or the worker recognized an additional hazard and chose to protect against it. That's "Above and Beyond."

Other Safe 2 behavior Examples:

- Demonstration of proper lifting technique
- Using machines to move materials and equipment.
- Using seatbelts
- Participating in safety inspections, safety meetings
- Leading Stretch & Flex
- Cleaning liquid spills and tracking their origin.
- Ability to explain LOTO, Safe Out, GHS, Hot Work, HazCom, etc.
- Worker 'triggers on the state' using the SafeStart™ system.
- Worker uses the "5-Whys" investigation technique for a quick assessment of near misses.
- Can you think of any other examples?
- **Name 2 more before proceeding.**

As the wearing of additional PPE is over and above the basic level of PPE it would therefore appear to warrant both attention and reinforcement since it is a behavior we should wish to see practiced in the workplace.

Other above and beyond safe behaviors might include things like: reporting near misses, demonstrating proper lifting technique, using equipment to move materials instead of by hand, seatbelt use, housekeeping another trade's messes, safety inspection participation, weekly safety focus walk participation, presenting the toolbox talk or safety meeting, cleaning up a fluid spill and tracking down its source;

leading the morning's Stretch & Flex, performing brother's keeper acts; a worker who can explain: excavation inspections, LOTO, Safe Out, Hot work, confined space permits; a worker who Triggers on the state (Safe Start)—Rushing, Fatigue, Frustration, Complacency; safety improvement, prevention of probably serious accident, safety leadership, Implementation of 360 Safety, reporting of OSHA non-compliance issues, etc.

Unsafe Behavior Identification

Consequences for unsafe behavior range from verbal warnings, minor disciplinary measures, or in extreme cases, termination. Unlike Safe behaviors, unsafe behaviors will be categorized into three groups:

The reason I am going through the types of behaviors and what I would do about them is because intent matters. If a worker was at least trying, that's something I can work with as far as behavior modification is concerned. On the other hand, if he doesn't give a white lab rat's butt about safety, then I don't want him on my project. So, let's dissect the types of unsafe behaviors and how to coach them (actually, coaching comes later).

Near misses are sometimes classified as lagging indicators and in one sense they are a report of an incident that happened but did not result in an injury or property damage. That's all well and good but I like to look at the 'reporting' aspect of near misses as the behavior we wish to encourage and report. This reporting aspect is a positive participative act that we want to encourage as this is an effective way to identify situations that could result in future injurious incidents.

- **Unsafe 1** behavior is somehow a dangerous act but does not normally warrant a severe punishment.

- **Unsafe 2** behavior is very dangerous behavior and seriously jeopardizes the safety of the workplace.
- **Unsafe 3** is blatant disregard of the existing safety regulations and usually warrants removal from the project.

Unsafe 1 Behaviors

Unsafe-1. The first group of unsafe behaviors are the behaviors that might at first glance indicate a lack of training or attention to detail on behalf of the worker. He or she may have had a momentary lapse in judgement and failed to don their gloves prior to dumping the trash after carrying the trash to break, for example (this resulted in 14 stitches).

More examples:

- A worker is leaning too far out on her ladder or standing on the second rung from the top of her ladder, for example.
- Multiple ladder safety issues (extension ladder not 36" above upper level, ladder not secured top or bottom, carrying materials up/down ladder, ladder on uneven surface, ladder angle too steep or not steep enough (4:1), ladder tag not being filled out indicating no daily inspection),
- Fall harness not signed, anchor of insufficient strength,
- incorrect lanyard for the situation—6-foot shock absorbing lanyard in use on a 10-foot Perry scaffold without guardrails which would allow worker to hit the floor,
- safety glasses all scratched up,
- Worker wearing safety glasses on forehead and nods his head to drop glasses down after seeing you walk around the corner—trust me, it happens all the time.

- Not wearing safety glasses because they keep fogging up (I use a 4:1 water to Dawn dish soap solution in a spray bottle. I carry it with me and clean off their glasses. This treatment usually lasts for a few days if done properly. Spray it on and let it dry. Then lightly buff off any bubbles).
- Not using goggles and a face shield with high pressure wash,
- not using the proper cut level of gloves,
- lack of proper dust control when cutting, grinding, drilling concrete or masonry,
- wearing a baseball cap under a hard hat,
- daisy chaining extension cords,
- damaged extension cords,
- cord too light duty for the task,
- using tools with guards removed or pinned back,
- not wearing a seat belt while operating equipment,
- not wearing metatarsal boots when required, etc. (or only wearing one metatarsal boot—yes, I have seen this).

What other Unsafe 1 behaviors can you think of? Stop and name 3 before proceeding.

As mentioned, there are literally thousands of situations that would fall into this category. What to do about them? We will get to that in the coaching section.

Unsafe 2 Behaviors

These behaviors are immediately dangerous to life and health (IDLH). This very likely could warrant the worker being sent home for a day or three.

Typical examples of Unsafe 2 behavior include:

- Welder failed to use PFAS (personal fall arrest system) when climbing onto steel beams that he was welding.
- Worker stood on mid-rail of scissor lift and was not tied off.
- Standing on top rung of A-frame ladder.
- An electrician leaving the ladder to perform work above the ceiling tiles without tying off.
- One worker pushing another in horseplay situations near unprotected rebar.
- A worker atop a 4-foot ladder next to a 3rd floor story window and not wearing fall protection.
- Worker failing to wear safety belt when operating machinery.
- Can you name 3 more before proceeding to the next section?

Before we jump to the next section, let's answer one question. Who should send the worker home? The supervisor is responsible for the safety enforcement of his crew and therefore he or she should be the one to send the worker home. That may be at the request of the safety professional, project manager, project superintendent, APM, Assistant superintendent, Plant manager, or fellow worker.

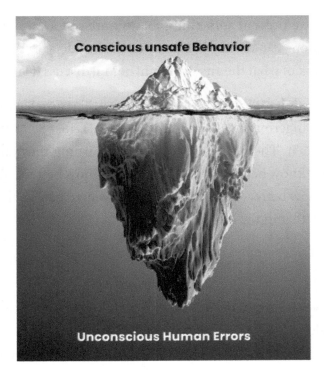

Conscious unsafe Behavior

Unconscious Human Errors

This Photo by Unknown Author is licensed under CC BY

Other than being a beautiful CGI image, much like NASA's CGI images of our Earth plane from "space", this depicts two types of decisions as they relate to behaviors in the workplace. There are Conscious Unsafe Behaviors which are decisions that are made knowing they are against the rules. Then there are the Unconscious Human Errors that are decisions made without thinking. We grab a box and lift without looking inside. Without doing a load size up first. Always perform a load size-up when performing a safe lift. That box could contain styrofoam or bolts and you won't know unless you look inside or try to nudge it to gauge it's weight.

Many Unsafe 2 behaviors tend to fall into these two groups. The point being made with this iceberg image, however, is that there are far more unconscious human errors than there are conscious ones.

So how do we prevent something that we are not aware of? That's a good question. It's already been answered, but do you remember or can you think of what the answer might be? I'll discuss it later on again.

Unsafe-2. Let's handle the second group next. These behaviors are immediately dangerous to life and health (IDLH). Just Send the worker home. That's it. The first time, they get no warning they just get sent home. They know better. Not, "They should know better." They absolutely do know better. There is a respectful way to handle this, and we will address that in the coaching section.

Here are a few examples of when workers have been justly sent home for the day.

- A welder exited the scissor lift to climb onto steel beams he was welding, and he was not wearing fall protection.
- A worker was standing on the top rung of his 8-foot A frame ladder to access plumbing above the tile ceiling and was not tied off.
- An electrician left his ladder to perform work above the ceiling tile and was not tied off.
- A welder climbed a ladder to undecked steel then proceeded to walk around with his beamer in one hand and his anchor strap in the other. He tied off and untied 3 times before I could get his attention.
- A plumber was 20 plus feet high sitting on the top rail of a scissor lift and not tied off. Workers were 20 feet high in a boom lift and not tied off.
- A worker scaling from point A to a lifeline on a cliff with a 75% slope and who was not practicing 100% tie off.
- Worker using a Perry scaffold with no guardrail, next to a 5-story window and not tied off.

- Worker pushing another worker in horseplay situation near unprotected rebar.
- Worker 4 rungs up on an 8' ladder next to an open 3rd story window without fall protection.
- Worker arguing with owner over pedestrian safety then bumping into (shoulder checking) the owner in a threatening manner (yes, this happened, and the worker was let go).

I could go on but suffice it to say these types of events, although no injury occurred, could have resulted in the serious injury or death of a worker.

Do I, as the safety professional, send them home? No, their supervisor is the one who sends them home at either my or the project superintendent's request ,or another ranking member of the management team. (Yes, we said this. Repetition is the mother of skill, remember?). It doesn't really matter who tells the supervisor, but we all need to be on the same sheet of music. So, depending on the potential severity of the act, and the worker's attitude, they may or may not get to return the next day. This leads us to the third group of unsafe acts.

Remember our beautiful iceberg? We are going to reuse it (reduce, re-use, & recycle, right?). The idea, as you probably know, is that there are far more near misses than actual minor injuries in the workplace while there are far more minor injuries than there are serious injuries and fatalities. (This was alluded to on page 27, if you recall). Therefore, if we can focus on eliminating the near misses and minor injuries, we should be able to greatly reduce the serious injuries and fatalities. From a behavioral-based safety perspective, the iceberg analogy translates thusly: The vast majority of all our behaviors are unconscious and that includes both safe and unsafe behaviors.

Typically, these unconscious acts are what we call habits or possibly instincts. The brain prefers habits over conscious acts because habits require much less energy to execute. It's like being on autopilot versus manning the helm. The short-handed sailor gets much more accomplished when he or she is not stuck at the helm. Likewise, the brain is more efficient when we create a habit for brushing our teeth, putting our pants on, tying our work boots, etc. than if we had to relearn each of these tasks every day. Can you imagine?

Unsafe 3 Behavior

Okay so the last, but certainly not the least of the unsafe behavior types is Unsafe 3. This level of safety behavior involves the worker demonstrating blatant disregard for the existing safety regulations resulting in a life-threatening exposure of the worker's safety and possibly that of surrounding people.

You should seriously reconsider tolerating the presence of such personnel on your project and in your workplace, even if it is a first offense. This behavior is not caused by a momentary lapse in judgement. You can tell by their reaction when you confront them. Do they show immediate remorse? Are they sorry or sorry they were caught? Does their reaction seem legit when they say they didn't know? Do they try to place the blame on others? You should be able to tell. Intent here is everything. Unsafe behaviors were categorized because the intent of the offense matters.

A person exhibiting Unsafe 3 level behavior is generally a person who cannot be rehabilitated with a single day off or through a written warning. This person knew it was against the rules to talk on his or her cell phone while operating a forklift, but they did it anyway. This is a person displaying clear and present danger to him or herself and to those around him or her. In this scenario, displaying Unsafe 3 behaviors, if things go south there is a high possibility of serious injury or death occurring on the site.

A behavior in the third group is when a worker displays a blatant and total disregard for his/her safety and/or the safety of others. We do not want and will not tolerate workers like this on our projects. This is not someone exhibiting a momentary lapse in judgement. This is not someone having a bad day. This is not someone we feel can be easily rehabilitated with a day off and/or a written warning. This is someone who displays a clear and present danger to themselves and others with a flippant attitude regarding safety policies that if things turn south, bad things happen, and people die. Some people are among the 10% who refuse to comply no matter what you do. It is what it is. Some who exhibit Unsafe 3 behaviors can be coached. Give them a day or three off and let them think about how badly they want to work here.

Examples:

- A worker walking or sitting on a parapet wall sans PFAS.
- A worker with serious anger management issues who resorts to violence in the workplace.
- A worker who needs to be reminded more than once to wear his harness when working at heights. Repeatedly refusing to wear a harness when "just moving a boom lift from here to there" is another example.

What other types of situations will get a worker permanently removed from my project? Horseplay that endangers life. That's a no brainer in my book. Working at heights with no thought for fall protection is another one. The key here being 'no thought for fall protection' because if a guy is wearing a harness and unhooks from one anchorage to move his lanyard to another anchorage, that just shows me he doesn't fully embrace the concept of 100% tie off. I'll probably warn him once and explain to him the concept, then if he does it again, send him home the second time. He can return the next day after showing documentation indicating retraining on the concept if he has a teachable attitude and if the superintendent, who likely knows him better than I do, agrees with him returning to work.

One critically important thing to consider is that all corrections and retraining must be in the worker's native language especially if his or her English language skills are somewhat challenged. We must ensure that workers are given ample opportunity to comprehend the training we are requiring of them. If you are the general contractor and not responsible for that worker's training, then doing your due diligence is to ensure that the training was performed in his/her native tongue. Require it in writing from the subcontractor. And it's not enough to just 'tell' the worker. Request that he explain it back to you. If you are in doubt, have him teach you the concept so that you know he understands the gravity of things. Have him demonstrate that he knows the skill. Okay. Enough on this.

What are some Unsafe 3 behavior examples?

- Allowing unauthorized persons onto job sites without the Safe 1 level of personal protective equipment. This includes untrained workers, new workers to the job who have yet to undergo site specific safety orientation and curious onlookers who wander in off the street asking questions like, "Whatcha buildin'?"
- Unprotected workers walking on or climbing over parapet walls, across undecked steel, or across decking that has no or inadequate guardrail system in place.

- Workers with serious anger-management problems who resort to violence to solve their issues.
- Unprotected workers jumping the gap between scaffold and building. (Always ensure your scaffolding completely covers the area to be worked in.)
- Workers who require regular reminding to wear harnesses or to install proper guardrails when working at heights.
- Crane operator talking on his cell phone while operating equipment unless it is to communicate with his signalman.

Spot the Behaviors

This Photo by Unknown Author is licensed under CC BY

Does the guy in the blue tee shirt look like he is properly equipped? Or that he even belongs there? Neither of them is wearing gloves. What else can you see?

Safe & Unsafe Behavior Levels Review

Behaviors in the workplace fall into one of five categories. There are two types, safe and unsafe but breaking those down further we can identify a total of five categories.

- Safe 1: meets minimum compliance requirements,
- Safe 2: above & beyond minimum compliance requirements,
- Unsafe 1: behavior that is serious but not a threat to life and not likely to cause serious injury.
- Unsafe 2: behavior that is serious and could be a threat to life and/ or cause serious injury to worker or others. (IDLH)
- Unsafe 3: behavior that if things go badly is likely to cause serious injuries or death and that warrants an employee to be removed immediately from the project.

CHAPTER 4
Identifying Types of Behaviors

Now that we understand both safe and unsafe behaviors, how can we effectively observe them in the workplace? What do we do with them once we have observed them?

In 1990 I was working for Potlatch Corporation in Lewiston, Idaho. It's had several names since I left in 2001. I began working there in 1988. My father, a journeyman welder and employee of the company since sometime in 1965, had just been asked to fill a position as the Safety Facilitator since the company was rolling out a relatively new behavioral-based safety program. There would be 12 Steering Committee members with individual specialties. My Dad more or less 'volun-told' me to serve on the committee because of my massage therapy and fitness background and my 'willingness' to participate. I immediately became the ergonomics chairperson. I took 2 weeks of general industry related ergonomics (CHAMPION) training and the steering committee members all received two weeks of training to becoming safety coaches and observers. "Observer" sounds too much like we were expected to spy on people, so I liked the term safety coach better. But it wasn't like that.

We didn't spy on workers but instead approached them and asked their permission if we could conduct a 10-minute observation. Rarely did a worker say no. Eventually dozens more workers were trained as safety observers, and we rotated out on the steering committee. We did thousands of observations, and the data was all gathered and put on computers. It was a very complicated system from where I sat. People complained of the long hours spent doing data entry. That part did not appeal to me.

This is how observations worked. We asked permission of a worker to do an observation. Then we spent about 10 minutes watching them do their jobs while checking boxes on a card and making comments. After which time we pulled the worker aside to review the observations. We always complimented them on areas of percieved strength (i.e., proper lifting technique used when you picked up that spent core) and we brought attention to areas of concern. We assured them they would remain anonymous. We never put their names on the cards. We asked if they had any safety concerns or suggestions.

Finally, we gave them a little trinket type gift with the safety program logo on it (a pen, a flashlight, a squishy stress ball, or other cheap memento of the occasion with, "P_O_W_E_R_" (Process of Workers Eliminating Risks) printed on it) and we dropped the observation card in a box where it was picked up later. Like I said, the training to be a safety coach was two weeks long and it was initially presented by a company called Behavioral Science Technology, Inc. (BST) if I am not mistaken. Psychology, coaching, tact, diplomacy, leading by example, OSHA standards, ergonomics, training, and many other topics were covered. It was a long time ago. But that was my first safety position and perhaps the mother of the safety incentive program you are studying now.

Sample Safety Observation Card

NEAR MISS / HAZARD ID

☐ Near Miss   ☐ Hazard Identification

DEFINITIONS

NEAR MISS - Any event, which under slightly different circumstances, may have resulted in injury or ill health of people, or damage or loss to property, materials or the environment.

HAZARD - Source or situation with a potential for harm in terms of injury, ill health, damage to property, damage to workplace and environment, or any other definitions as set out by regulations and codes.

Reported by: _____

Date Reported: _____ Job #: _____

Check All Applicable   ☐ Unsafe Act   ☐ Unsafe Condition

     ☐ Unsafe Equipment   ☐ Unsafe Use Of Equipment

Description of Near Miss or Hazard:

What was the potential consequence?:

Recommendations to prevent recurrence?:

Corrective action taken:

Corrective action taken by: _____

Date of corrective action: _____

BEHAVIOURAL BASED OBSERVATION

OBSERVATION CARD

INITIAL ACTIONS	SAFE	UNSAFE	N/A
EYES ON TASK	☐	☐	☐
NOT RUSHING	☐	☐	☐
BALANCE, TRACTION, GRIP	☐	☐	☐

LINE OF FIRE	SAFE	UNSAFE	N/A
BODY POSITION (FALLING, STRUCK BY, PINCH POINTS)	☐	☐	☐
PPE (REQUIRED, ADEQUATE, GOOD CONDITION, WORN PROPERLY)	☐	☐	☐
SCREEN, GUARDS, RAILS	☐	☐	☐
ISOLATION (LOCKOUT)	☐	☐	☐

BODY MECHANICS	SAFE	UNSAFE	N/A
LIFTING, BENDING, TWISTING	☐	☐	☐
REPETITIVE MOTIONS	☐	☐	☐
REACHING, PULLING, PUSHING (EXCESSIVE FORCE)	☐	☐	☐
STANDING, SITTING, KNEELING (LONG PERIODS)	☐	☐	☐
COMFORTABLE (VS AWKWARD POSITION)	☐	☐	☐

PROCEDURES & STANDARDS	SAFE	UNSAFE	N/A
Up-to-date, Understood	☐	☐	☐
Followed	☐	☐	☐
Orderliness (HOUSEKEEPING, STORAGE, ACCESS)	☐	☐	☐

TOOLS & EQUIPMENT	SAFE	UNSAFE	N/A
Safe Condition (PRE-USE INSPECTION, INSPECTION)	☐	☐	☐
Correct For Task	☐	☐	☐
Safe Use	☐	☐	☐

SIGNIFICANT ASPECTS OF OBSERVATION & DISCUSSION

Including what task was observed, employees comfort level, ideas for improving task and job, overall reception, follow-up items, etc.:

☐ FOLLOW-UP REQUIRED   SEVERITY POTENTIAL (If Applicable)
(Only applicable if unsafe actions were observed)
   ☐ Level 3 - Major Injury or Fatality
   ☐ Level 2 - Lost Time Injury or Medical Aid
   ☐ Level 1 - Minor Injury or First Aid

Job #: _____ Date: _____ Client: _____

Observers Name(s): _____

These types of cards are fine for their designed purpose but for an effective behavior-based safety program, we don't need all of this. It's rather time consuming and takes an army of observers, and data entry personnel to implement effectively.

Spot the behaviors

What are the safe and unsafe behaviors going on here?

Spot the behaviors

Safe & Unsafe

Spot the behaviors

Safe & Unsafe

Spot the behaviors

Safe & Unsafe

Spot the behaviors

Safe & Unsafe

CHAPTER 5
Safety Card Benefits

Chris Hermann wrote: "Formal Performance Management Systems will, by virtue of their structure, never be spontaneous enough to catch employees using role-model behavior in day-to-day activities but these systems have a crucial role to play in educating the workforce about not only the thrust of the business but also the role that they are expected to play in organizational success." (*The Ultimate Guide to Employee Recognition Programs—Learn What Rewards Work and What Don't Work*, 2011).

- Compared to formal performance management systems, the Safety Card Incentive Program is more versatile and easier to implement. All you need to do while walking the job site is carry a few blank safety cards in your pocket and observe workers from a distance. When you see them doing something right, you approach and work your positive reinforcement magic.

Benefits

- Uses specificity to reinforce safe behaviors,
- Ties positivity to the safe acts and reinforces those acts,
- Fosters worker engagement,
- Allows workers to know that you care about them,
- Identifies unsafe work conditions, procedures,
- Tracks safe behaviors and identifies behaviors not being tracked.

What is a Safety Card?

With all this talk about Safety Card Incentive Program, what the heck is a safety card? Is it a numbered raffle ticket? Nope! Nothing like that. I don't use those because they aren't personal, and they are tiny and too easy to lose.

The other type of observation card was shown earlier. It's long and has many boxes to check. It's more of an overall safe behavior audit than a spot check of one or two specific behaviors. With the focus on 30 behaviors, how is the worker supposed to remember the one or two main things you'd like him or her to focus on? It's just not going to happen. Most checklists detract from the Safety Card Incentive Program objectives that the process be:

- Specific,
- Consistent,
- Immediate and,
- Personal.

The safety cards we use in SCIP are the size of a standard business card. They can contain lined spaces where specific behaviors, names, etc. can be written down. This method supports the need to be Specific, Personal, Immediate, & Consistent.

I was speaking recently with one of our project senior superintendents (Chris) who recently adopted this safety incentive program. He told me that when he walked out on the project that morning, one of the forklift operators made eye contact with him as he tugged on his seatbelt. The superintendent gave the operator a thumbs up and mouthed the words, "Good job!". It was what happened next that proved to me the benefit of this program. The worker made a gesture with one hand for the superintendent to give him something. What was that something? The superintendent instantly knew that what the operator wanted was a safety card for wearing his seatbelt. He was asking for a reward for his performance of a safe behavior. This is exactly the objective of the safety card program, to have workers keep safety behavior top of mind even if he seeks attention or reward for that safety behavior. Should we be concerned that the worker is requesting a reward?

Honestly, it matters not that workers seek a reward for obeying the safety rules that they are required to obey. That's not what's important. We are developing habits. What is important is that the workers go home safely at the end of each day and if we must coax them into complying with the rules by giving them a little reward, until that behavior becomes habitual, that's just fine by me. The alternative, and the old school safety cop method of enforcement was that the superintendent or safety manager yelled at an operator for not wearing his seatbelt. The operator put it on as long as the safety manager was around, but he 'forgot' to put it on when returning from break. It either slipped his mind or it was intentionally not used. If the operator did happen to have it on, the superintendent said nothing. But that was life before SCIP.

Let's fast forward to today's superintendent or safety manager using our SCIP system. This operator knows there's a chance his safety gal might walk around the corner seeking to reinforce seatbelt use. The operator knows that he must be wearing the seatbelt when the safety manager first spots him on his forklift. If he puts it on after seeing the safety manager, then no card will be given (a card he can later use as a raffle ticket in the weekly drawing). So, the forklift operator is more inclined to keep his seatbelt on more often.

So, what exactly is a safety card? A safety card is the size of a business card. We said that already. How the cards are designed is up to personal preference. You might choose to list safe behaviors with boxes that are checked by the observer who also writes his or her name and the employee's name on the front of the card. In my opinion, that's not a great idea. I know because we tried it. You can't possibly print enough behaviors on a business card to cover all the situations you might encounter in the workplace. So, instead of a long list of behaviors (which looks very cluttered on a biz-card sized piece of paper) perhaps you may choose to design your cards like the ones I will show you here, with space to write observed behaviors as they arise. This second method is a little slower when filling out cards on the spot but gives the observer/coach more freedom. There is not unlimited space on a business card to print the myriad of behaviors you will encounter in the workplace. On the other hand, it may help your observers to have a list of potential behaviors to be on the lookout for. The back of each card can be left blank, or you could print the "2 steps to save a life" or some other significant messaging, so as not to waste the space.

The safety card serves several purposes. First and foremost, it reinforces a safe behavior, but it can also be used to teach a new skill.

Safety person: "Hey Judy, I noticed how perfect your lifting technique was just now when you picked up that bin. Your feet were shoulder width apart. Your back was nice and straight, and you were looking straight ahead, not with your head bent down like some folks. You used your legs and not your back to lift. Good job. So, I want to give you a Safety Card. And, I have one question for you. Was your core engaged?"

Judy: "My what?"

Safety person: "Your core. Can you describe to me how to properly engage your core?"

(If she doesn't know, take a moment to explain it to her then have her demonstrate).

Safety person: "Well, here's your safety card that you can use in our weekly/monthly drawing! So, good luck and again, I want to say thanks. Nicely done!"

This is the main purpose of the safety card program, to tie the reward to the safe act and reinforce that act. Remember that for positive reinforcement to work it must be specific, personal, immediate, and consistently applied.

The Back of the Card

On the back of each card can be printed something useful like this '2-Steps to Save a Life' with clip art images to not waste the space. I put this together but you are welcome to use it.

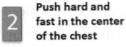

TWO STEPS TO SAVE A LIFE

1 Call
911

2 Push hard and
fast in the center
of the chest

Chapter 5: Safety Card—Benefits

- A card that is the size of a business card with a design based on company preferences
- Easy to carry
- Inexpensive to print

How can we get some safety cards?

Have someone in the office design a card for you in PowerPoint. Save it as a pdf. Open a Vistaprint account online and upload your design. You can use whichever printing outfit you like but I have used Vistaprint for over 10 years and the one time they sent me the wrong thing, (there was coating on the cards or something which makes them hard to write on with a ball point pen) they immediately resent the correct order and let me keep the coated cards (I just used a Sharpie on those). I don't benefit from you using Vistaprint. It's not like I own any stock in the company, but they have worked well for me. (If you can't figure it out, contact me and I can walk you through the process).

If you don't know how to use PowerPoint, go to the "University of YouTube™" and search for what you want. It's probably there. You can also design cards (and many other products) in Vistaprint on their website. I spend about $75 for 1500 cards. They last a few months.

Tracking behaviors:

After the raffle (see below) save the safety cards and record which behaviors were observed. Keep track of what types of behaviors you are noticing. As different members of your management team hand out cards, each person is going to notice different things. The person tracking all the cards can take notice if certain behaviors are being over-observed while others are not being observed enough and make recommendations to the management team going forward to be on the lookout for this or for that safe behavior.

After you record the behaviors, you can destroy the cards and toss them in the dumpster. If you don't want to do that, you can start a safety card wall of fame and use a pushpin to stick them to a board. Any card with a hole in it becomes 'expired' and unable to be used in subsequent drawings. If you are going to trash them, be sure to tear them in half or draw a big X on them with a marker so you know they can't be reused.

Role play:

- You and a partner will role play the observer and the worker being observed.
- The observer noticed the worker is properly tied off in a boom lift, but said worker is not wearing any safety glasses.

- Give the worker a safety card for properly tying off and remind them of the importance of always using proper eye protection.
- You might mention any risks associated with not wearing glasses while operating a boom lift.

Teach and/ or Reinforce a New Skill

This Photo by Unknown Author is licensed under CC BY

If you are reading this at home, then go practice with a family member. Try it first without the family member knowing what you are up to so you can gauge his or her honest reaction. Approach that person, call them by name and tell them what a fine job they are doing at this or that specific task. Express how much you appreciate what they are doing. Be specific about the task and the way they are doing it. If it's your daughter and she is washing dishes, tell her you really appreciate how clean she gets the dishes. How little of a mess she makes while washing or that she is doing a great job of drying them, or not breaking them, or whatever. Don't say, "I appreciate that you always do a good job" at whatever the behavior is. That's too generic.

Just acknowledge the exact behavior on this specific time. Then, ask her if she needs anything from you and again thank her and go back to what you were doing before (reading this book, presumably). Did you notice how she reacted? Did she smile? Did she scrunch up her eyebrows wondering what you were up to? Ha, ha, ha. You'll get that at first but after the workers (or your kids) realize this is something that they can benefit from, you'll have them hook, line, and sinker.

Your son (or daughter) is out mowing the lawn. Take a tall glass of lemonade out to the porch and get his attention. Have him shut down the mower and call him over. Hand him the lemonade and tell him how proud you are that he is paying so much attention to the corners and edges and making sure to make straight lines with the mower. His attention to detail is impeccable and you tell him so. Thank him for wearing hearing protection, gloves, long pants, shoes that cover his toes and safety glasses. Ask him how he's doing. He says, "It's freaking hot, Dad." Say, "I know wearing all that safety stuff is hot and I hope you know how important your hands, eyes, legs, feet, ears, and face are to me, so I wanted to show my appreciation to you by bringing you this lemonade. Thank you, son." Now give him a hug, or shake his hand, and ask if he has any questions for you.

Role Play: Observer and Worker

Select one behavior to reinforce and one behavior to teach.

Remember you are going to reinforce one behavior here using the safety card but there is also another behavior, an unsafe one, which you want to correct. (Hint: it's red and on the ground with no handle or guard). Like my hint?

Badge
of
Honour

Believe it or not, I have known guys who took their cards home to show them off to their wives. "Look, honey. I got this at work today for being safe. I know you understand that my job is a little dangerous, but I can assure you that I am doing all I can to come home in one piece to you and the kids every night." We never know how far and wide that ripple, in the pond of life, will travel.

In some ways, a safety card is a badge of honor that a worker can carry around. Or he or she might take it home and set it on the dresser. Maybe a spouse finds it in the laundry and asks what is a safety card? (It reads "Safety Card" in bright red letters). Then the worker can beam with pride as he tells his significant other how the site safety manager walked up to him and called his name in front of "the crew". He can tell how he was a bit nervous until he heard, "Thank you and congrats! I want to give you a safety card for going out of your way to caution another worker about using a quickie saw without wearing a face shield," or whatever the reason. If the worker carries the card in his or her wallet, he or she is reminded of the experience each time the card is seen. More behavior reinforcement.

More benefits to using Safety Cards:

- More eyes looking for hazardous conditions and safe/ unsafe behaviors,
- Cards are tossed into a bucket at weekly safety meetings where they become raffle tickets,
- The card is a true demonstration of behavior reinforcement through focus,
- Turn your safety culture around on its head!
- Make safety fun at your workplace,
- Reduce/ eliminate incidents,

- Track safe behaviors & determine where to focus next.

Safety Cards are not handed out like candies on Halloween. They must be earned. But don't be so stingy with them that you only hand out 2 or 3 a week. How fun will that raffle be? I recommend weekly drawings (raffles) over monthly ones due to jobsite turnover and so workers don't have to wait so long for their public recognition and chance to win.

How else can SCIP benefit your work environment?

- It can help to boost self-esteem and confidence of the workforce. When an authority figure or someone you respect takes a few moments out of his or her day to compliment you on your work ethic, that can leave a lasting impression of positivity and good feelings.
- Public recognition before co-workers encourages workers to always be compliant in case a safety observer walks around the corner.
- A word of caution: Be very aware of workers who have not been getting any cards. Try to make sure you observe them too, doing something safe. Otherwise, this group can become disgruntled and might speak poorly of the Safety Card Incentive Program which could work to derail the program.
  - o Work with their supervisor if they are not easily accessible for observations.
  - o Encourage their coworkers to nominate them for safety cards.

CHAPTER 6

Safety Cards and Positive Reinforcement

This Photo by Unknown Author is licensed under CC BY

For positive reinforcement to be most efficient, it should be specific, personal, immediate, and consistent. (You might read this again and you might have read it at least twice already. Do you think it's important?).

Specific

Identify the specific behavior at that precise moment instead of general behaviors over a longer period. The goal of each encounter should be to identify and reinforce specific behaviors. Do not give a safety card out for general safe behavior but instead give one card for one or two specific behaviors that you desire to reinforce. Saying things like, "You're such a safe worker. I'm going to give you a safety card today because you have been so good all week!" This is wrong. This does nothing at all to reinforce any specific behavior. It might make both of you feel good generally, but that's not the ultimate objective of this program. The aim of each encounter ought to be about identifying and reinforcing specific behaviors and tying a feeling of positivity to that specific behavior. It's not recognition of a worker's general safety attitude. That's what quarterly luncheons are for. Such generic accolades send the message to this worker that each time he took a shortcut, and you didn't see him, he got away with it. It tells him that you appreciate the fact that he didn't get hurt. It conveys the message that you care about him, and you appreciate the fact that he makes a point of wearing his PPE and being a generally safe employee. It speaks volumes to the other workers who were just as safe as this guy but did not happen to be in your crosshairs and therefore did not get a safety card and it tells them that being safe only matters if the boss sees you. None of these are messages we should be spreading.

Also, do not wait until a worker has been 100% safe for a week or a few days before seeking an opportunity to reward him/ her with a safety card. Giving the card as a reward is to entice or encourage safe behaviors, not to acknowledge a perfect history of performance.

I once had a superintendent who said, "I'm not giving these guys any safety cards this week. Not until they straighten up!" I had to explain to him the safety cards are there to help him help them straighten up.

It also bares mentioning that the safety card program is tied 100% to leading indicators and never to lagging indicators. For those who do not know, leading indicators are events that tend to prevent an injury while lagging indicators are post event measures like the number of injuries in a year. Some leading indicators are, safe behavior observations, participating in safety meetings, safety inspections, stretch & flex, etc. Leading indicators are going out of your way to stop a near miss before it happens, or when a worker tells you about a hole cover that looks damaged. Behaviors precede consequences so if we want to eliminate negative consequences like injuries, then we need to replace unsafe behaviors with safe behaviors. Is this making sense yet? I hope so! ☺

This means that safety cards are earned when an employee performs safety related behaviors as opposed to being earned for sustaining "no injuries". As we all know, rewarding employees for not reporting injuries may tempt employees to not report injuries unless safeguards are put in place to discourage this behavior. Other than this brief mention, we are not going to discuss this topic as it does not relate to our safety incentive program.

What we do hope to gain by recognizing and rewarding specific safe behaviors is changed behavior through affirmative reinforcement that is accompanied by a good feeling. We are seeking real learning which is best achieved by the implementation of a positively reinforced leading indicator rewards-based system. Say that five times fast.

Positive reinforcement is most effective when it is **specific, personal, immediate, and consistent** (Repetition is the mother of skill). The Safety Card is most effective in producing a strong correlation between antecedent and consequence, between the behavior being reinforced and the reward, when very little time passes between the observed behavior and receipt of said reward. The longer we wait before giving the reward the less effective is the motivation when reinforcing a behavior. Imagine giving a dog a treat 30 minutes after you got him to sit, or worse yet, the next day. It wouldn't make much sense to the dog and likewise, the practice of delayed reward doesn't correlate very strongly with humans.

This is a reinforcement technique that identifies a specific behavior at a precise moment rather than waiting for general patterns over a longer period.

Remember that positive reinforcement is the most powerful motivation. Give Safety Cards out for specific behaviors that you desire to reinforce in the organization. If you are working with a subcontractor in construction who might be working under a corrective action plan due to failure to pass your company's stringent minimum safety standards, get familiar with that sub's corrective action plan action items. Those are their problem areas, and you can become instrumental in helping them turn these perceived weaknesses into strengths.

Remember. Be specific to the behavior you want to reinforce or modify. "Thanks for wearing a face shield while using the chop saw to cut metal framing."

Not, "Thanks for not getting hurt today!" Or, "Thanks for being safe!" Both are nice things to say, but they don't reinforce any specific behaviors.

Leading indicators are actions meant to prevent an incident from occurring while lagging indicators are post-behavior events/ results after the occurrence of an injury, for example. These are metrics which we measure, and they can give us a decent perspective of what has happened in the past, but they are not necessarily indicative of future events. As mentioned earlier, for positive reinforcement to be most effective, it must be specific, immediate, personal, and consistent. Trust me, I realize I sound like a broken record, but remove any one of those attributes and the whole system falls apart.

Personal

It is not recommended to hand out cards to larger groups (5+) of workers at one time. Give the safety card on the spot to one or a very few workers who were involved with a specific task. Effective safety communication during a crane operation could be an example of when a handful of workers were involved in a safe act. A specific example of this would be if the operator lost sight of the load and his coms went down so he stopped the load. The signalman then found another way to communicate with the operator. Using each person's name is meant to make them feel special and appreciated as individuals, not as one less significant member of a larger group. Do not hand out several cards to a group of workers and tell them to write their own names on the cards. That's not very personal and it's just lazy on your part. Remember that any job worth doing is worth doing well. Do your job well and use their name.

Give cards to each specific worker who was involved in a particular task so that you can make him or her feel valued. Shake each worker's hand. Look him or her in the eye and tell them thank you. Let them know you appreciate that they care about going home to their family every day in one piece. Don't joke and say that it makes your job easier by having to do less paperwork. It's true but it's bad form. Also, giving the card to large groups could make those who were heavily involved to feel as being less significant members of the group. It diminishes the value of a card when one guy worked more safely than the other guy and they both got a card for the same thing.

Always learn and use the worker's name prior to recognizing their safe behavior and before handing them their safety card. Write their name on the card. In other words, try to get the guy's name before you approach him. If you can't then as soon as you approach him, introduce yourself and get his name. Write it down on the card as he is saying it to you. I usually say something like, "Hi there. How's it going? I'm Rick the safety guy. Can I get your name? It's nothing bad." If they are aware of SCIP they are happy to give you, their name. If they are new to the job and don't know what you are doing, now is the perfect time to explain SCIP to them. Use the worker's name in the conversation. Write the behavior on the card. Write your name on the card or if another worker nominated someone for a safety card, then write the person who nominated the worker in place of your name. Names matter.

When conversing with the employee, use his or her name as a sign of respect. The safe behavior of the worker should also be written on the card, as well as the name of the observer. A name matters and that is why you should make this event personal. Using their name shows you care, and it tends to lower communication barriers. If I feel like you care about me, I am less wary of your intentions regarding me.

When someone uses our name, it makes us feel just a little bit special, especially if that someone is an authority figure. So, when you hear the worker's name, repeat it out loud. Write it on the card. Use it several times, almost to the point where it seems like you are overusing their name. Trust me, it will help you learn it. If you forget, don't be afraid to say, "Dang it. What was your name again? I'm going to keep asking you until I learn it so don't be offended. Ha, ha, ha," or something like that. Humor deflects your awkwardness and slight embarrassment so use it if you need to. Then if you don't see that worker for two weeks and you forget his name, you've already set the stage for needing to re-ask his name. Trust me when I tell you that the worker will appreciate your efforts to learn his or her name. And that appreciation will go a long way to getting workers to want to please you by complying with safety policies.

Having said that, there are tricks to remembering things and even people's names. Here is a short article on 7 tips to remember people's names. My favorite is number 5. What's yours? https://www.newsmax.com/FastFeatures/memory-tricks-remember-name/2016/06/13/id/733660/

Along these lines, it is crucial to show you care about each worker. Tell them you appreciate him or her. Express your gratitude. Tell him or her thank you for demonstrating such and such safe behavior. There is little more motivating than hearing someone you respect tell you how proud they are of you. I am reminded of the times during my teenage years when my father would pull me aside to tell me how proud of me, he was at that time for the good choices I was making. I still remember how that made me feel. It inspired me to do better because I did not wish to disappoint him.

Ideally, a safety professional or superintendent builds rapport and earns worker respect over time. Be sincere and genuine in giving praise. Praise the behavior, not the individual. Make the interface short and sweet. Be sensitive to cultural differences. A handshake or a fist bump as the safety card is given, can go a long way.

Incidentally, be professional, thorough, and brief when dishing out constructive criticism. I like to use the Oreo™ cookie or sandwich approach (more on that later). But don't treat the worker like a small child by speaking down to him/her. And if possible, do not shame a worker in front of his peers. There is no quicker way to lose his or her respect. It is also of paramount importance, after having corrected a worker's behavior, reminding him to don PPE, for example, to circle back around and acknowledge and maybe even thank him for keeping it on. Notice if the glasses are scratched, dirty, foggy, or otherwise difficult to see through and make it a point to see that he gets clean, unscratched glasses or the right gloves and that they are not worn through.

These acts of kindness show that you genuinely care, and that demonstration will go a long way. There is an LDS scripture that comes to mind.

41 No power or influence can or ought to be maintained by virtue of the priesthood, only by persuasion, by long-suffering, by gentleness and meekness, and by love unfeigned;

42 By kindness, and pure knowledge, which shall greatly enlarge the soul without hypocrisy, and without guile—

43 Reproving betimes with sharpness, when moved upon by the Holy Ghost; and then showing forth afterwards an increase of love toward him whom thou hast reproved, lest he esteem thee to be his enemy; (Doctrine & Covenants 121: 41-43).

Instead of the word 'priesthood' substitute 'authority' and this is predominantly what I go by in the field. If his glasses are foggy, offer to spray them for him and give them back all clean and anti-fogged (4:1 water to Dawn™ dishsoap in a little spray bottle, the bottle which you can find online). He will appreciate it and may even ask you for your anti-fog spray next time he sees you. "Hey Rick, do you have any of that anti-fog spray on you?"

Immediate

Nobody wants to wait eons to be recognized for doing something right. Prolonging the period between moments of recognition weakens the bond between performing a safe act and the good feeling experienced for being rewarded (for doing the safe behavior).

What we are combatting here is the positive reward a worker gets when he or she performs unsafe behavior and gets away with it without getting caught and without being injured. That cycle is repeated endlessly in the workplace and that is what we are fighting against. So, in the beginning, we need to dole out positive reinforcement as if we were giving air to a drowning man. Frequently and plenty of it.

The quicker the positive reinforcement reward (safety card and your expression of gratitude) is to the demonstration of safe behavior, the stronger is the good feeling associated with that behavior and the more likely that behavior will be repeated. Wait too long and they most likely won't remember performing that safe behavior.

An immediate reward happens in the field when you give out the card followed by a public recognition (reward) on Friday, which reinforces the first positive reinforcement (private recognition) earlier in the week. As mentioned earlier, for positive reinforcement to be most effective, it must be specific, immediate, personal, and consistent.

Consistent

Consistency is a resourceful tool in motivation. However, it must be appreciated that safety cards are meant for reinforcement of a behavior and not to be used as crutching tools. What I try to do here is to spread out the period of the reinforcement schedule. You should be able to tell when a worker needs help learning to make a safe behavior a habit and when you are being used.

In the beginning of the motivation process, the operant conditioning reinforcement schedule, more frequent reward processes are instrumental in helping the subject grasp most of the intention of the motivation. To reiterate, the motivation is the 'why'. Why are they motivated to perform safely? With time, you can relax some of the incentive techniques as the subject continues to grasp the motivation and acts as intended. Before then, consistency is key in reinforcing a behavior. Then you can shift the focus and safety cards as rewards onto the Safe 2 behaviors while rewarding the Safe 1 behaviors with words of affirmation and gratitude. You will have to almost wean them from safety cards for Safe 1 behaviors but tell them you'll give them a safety card for wearing their safety glasses (Safe 1 behavior) if they tell you each time, they see you that they are doing that behavior. This still makes them responsible for their safety and it indicates to you that this safe behavior is top of mind for them. This way you can give verbal rewards each time you see them and a safety card near the end of the week for the same behavior. You can give cards out for other behaviors too but this way you keep reinforcing the safe behavior that replaced the previously problematic behavior if need be. Eventually you will tell them that you aren't giving cards out for Safe 1 behaviors anymore because they have done so well with those that they are not graduated up to Safe 2 behaviors. Tell them it's time to take off the training wheels.

Consistency is important; however, we need to keep in mind that the safety cards are a tool to be used to reinforce a behavior and not to become a crutch. So, what is the difference?

When reinforcing desired behaviors in a dog, for example, we initially give one reward for each time the dog responds positively to our command. If we say 'sit' and he sits, he gets a treat and a "Good boy!" If he doesn't sit, he gets nothing. After he learns to respond to the command, we can begin to periodically withhold the snack portion of the reward while maintaining the words of affirmation. "You're a good boy, Bear!"

Eventually, we can withdraw the words of affirmation also. Occasionally we can still give words of affirmation and even a snack, but the dog won't always expect it.

This is not to infer that workers are like dogs in any way shape or form. Not at all, but the principles of operant conditioning do transfer. The reinforcement of safety behaviors is possible with a reward-based system, but it does not have to become a one for one trade every time, or even at all, but it should be noted that perhaps in the beginning more frequent rewards might help to bring about the desired safety response.

This Photo by Chelsea Laird reprinted with permission

Conversely, this does not mean that we should completely remove the reward system after full compliance has been obtained. To do this would surely encourage backsliding to previous behaviors.

Eventually, we can withdraw the regularity of expressing words of affirmation. Occasionally we can still give words of affirmation and even a snack, but the dog won't always expect it.

If I tell the workers in the morning toolbox talk that I am going to be handing out safety cards for safe lifting techniques that day, because that was the topic of the morning toolbox talk, then two hours later when I'm doing rounds, and at first when I walk up to a small group of workers maybe nobody will remember. But if subtly prompted, several of them may suddenly find the "need" to squat down and pick something up. I have literally observed this behavior scores of times over the years that I have been using safety cards to reinforce safety and health related behaviors. It works. It matters not if the need to lift something is real or inspired by my presence. What matters is that they desire to demonstrate safe lifting technique for me. I know they might be doing it only to earn a safety card. That's okay because the more times a person practices a safe lift, for whatever reason, the stronger that person's legs will become, the easier lifting will be, and the more likely he or she is to perform a proper lift when nobody is looking. That is changed behavior and that is the best definition of learning.

The Sandwich Approach or the Oreo™ Cookie approach as I used to call it. I don't eat Oreo™ Cookies any more though because I recently discovered the meaning of HEK 293 and "natural flavors" and now I won't touch them with a ten-foot pole. But the concept still applies. There is something on the outside and something different on the inside. Hmm, I'm going to use the sandwich analogy here. Let's say it's a liver and onions sandwich. I pick that because probably most folks wouldn't much care for the taste of a liver and onions sandwich. Although they would be very healthy for you if served on sourdough bread. Learn to use the sandwich approach when pointing out unsafe behaviors while at the same time recognizing safe behaviors. This approach enables the worker to feel good for the recognition of a safe behavior while at the same time leaving him reconsidering the unsafe behavior.

If, for instance, a worker demonstrated mostly proper lifting skills, but kept his weight centered in the balls of his feet (rather than in his heels where it should be) then praising the worker for clearing materials aways from his travel route, doing a load size up, bending his knees, keeping his eyes front and his back straight and core engaged would all be areas of positive constructive criticism that would make him feel good to have them each mentioned. Then slip in the bit about, "Oh and I don't know if you know this but it's important to keep your weight centered in your heels so that you don't blow your knee out. Did you know that?"

It might be a good idea to research this and explain why it's important to center the weight in the heels. (Hint: it puts less pressure on the patellar ligament).

There are times and ways to criticize and coach unsafe behaviors. If the safe behavior you are rewarding is accompanied by another not so safe behavior, it is okay to point out the unsafe behavior but as mentioned, use the sandwich approach when doing so. The purpose is to leave the worker feeling good about the experience so to briefly mention the mostly safe lifting technique only to spend five minutes chastising her for NOT keeping her weight in her heels, is not going to leave her with a good overall sense of the experience. If most of the lifting was correct but you want to use the opportunity to remind the worker to keep her weight in her heels versus in the balls of her feet, then describe the correct aspects of her lift first, followed briefly with something like, "And I know it is easy to forget, but remember to keep your weight in your heels as you lift, not in the balls of your feet. Here, let's do it together for practice. We wouldn't want you to blow out your knee now, would we?"

Say that it might feel a little awkward the first few times but that it will become easier with practice, just like most skills we learn. Then demonstrate and have her follow along with her weight in her heels so she gets the chance to develop the muscle memory for this behavior. This extra coaching can help to motivate the worker in correcting errant behavior. Now let's talk about coaching!

CHAPTER 7
Coaching Techniques

Preparation

- To be adept at safe behavior observation you really should get your OSHA 10 & 30 and that's just for starters.
- Study ergonomics and the various OSHA standards that are applicable to your industry.
- Read books like:
  - o "How to Win Friends and Influence People" by Dale Carnegie
  - o "The Seven Habits of Highly Effective People" by Stephen R. Covey
  - o "The One Minute Manager" by Ken Blanchard and Spencer Johnson or
  - o "Spiritual Roots of Human Relations" also Stephen R. Covey
- Learn what to look for and how to speak to people at their level and not down to them if you wish to be respected.

Observation Skills

- Compliment in areas where you can observe strengths (example; proper lifting techniques when transferring materials from one place to another)
- Bring attention to areas of concern while assuring them that their identity shall remain anonymous ~ if possible.
- Seek opinion from them in case they may have safety concerns.
- Seek first to understand, then seek to teach.
    - " Why are you doing this or that?" "Can you think of a safer way?" "What about trying this way instead?"
    - "If possible" means unless IDLH, repeat unsafe behavior, or negative attitude are factors.

Caring

It is instrumental to show you care about each worker that you encounter.

- Caring involves asking about them, using their name and expressing appreciation of a job well done.
- Be generous with Gratitude as a Coaching Technique.
- Say 'thank you" for even the little accomplishments that they achieve.
- If it sounds corny because we are big strong tough construction workers, or whatever, then preface your expression of gratitude with something like, "This might sound a bit corny, but I do appreciate the fact that you care about safety. I wish everyone would pay as much attention to housekeeping, keeping exits clear, wearing proper PPE for the task, etc. as you do." There are ways to make it not feel so awkward.

- A small expression of gratitude from a satisfied supervisor can go a long way to motivate a worker toward excellence.
- <u>Example:</u> From time to time, during the author's teenage years, his father would pull him aside and tell his teenage son how proud he was of him for a particular decision that was made. (Dad's encouraging words still ring in his ears to this day.)
- Gratitude makes a worker feel inspired and try harder not to disappoint.

Rapport as a Coaching Technique

Hopefully the safety professional has been building rapport over time and has been showing the workers that he cares about them so there is a measure of respect there. Be sincere and genuine in giving praise.

Praise the behavior and not the individual. Make the interface short and sweet, like a cupcake (or Kaycee, my granddaughter). Be sensitive to cultural differences, but a firm handshake with solid eye contact, as the safety card is handed over, is the cream cheese icing on that cupcake. Other thoughts about rapport.

- Rapport helps in earning respect over time.
- Always remain sincere and genuine in the pursuit of building rapport.
- In case a worker does something good, praise the action, not the actor.
- During your interaction with the workers, make the session short but memorable.
- You work in an environment characterized by cultural differences; be sensitive to cultural differences if possible.
- Offering a handshake or a fist pump as you reward behavior with a safety card goes a long way in building rapport.

This Photo by Unknown Author is licensed under CC BY

The Sandwich Approach

I just realized I am using plenty of food references. I hope it's not just before lunch time for you as you are ingesting this material, feasting on the words in your book. ☺

If you are wondering why this guy keeps mentioning this Sandwich Approach, it's because I use it all the time. It is very effective at giving me the opportunity to correct errant behavior while sandwiching that criticism between some feel good stuff. We need to know that when you come in guns blazing with your safety rules and regulations that worker's mind just glazed over. He hears you but he isn't really listening. Not always, but often this is the case. Add the fact that you don't speak his native tongue and you've really got a communication barrier. He will smile and nod his head and don his glasses but since you didn't ask him why he wasn't wearing them in the first place (seek first to understand then seek to teach) you have shown you don't care about his problems and so why should he listen to anything you have to say?

If I were doing footnotes, this would be a footnote. I'm going to take a side bar, sort of here and admit that this "Seek first to understand, then seek to teach" phrase I keep repeating was inspired by a Stephen R. Covey quote. He wrote, "Seek first to understand, then to be understood," and although I like that, a lot, 'teaching' to me denotes understanding on behalf of the student. If your student is not understanding what you are presenting, then you aren't teaching effectively and hence you are not teaching at all. Teaching is to convey a thought, idea, theory, principle, behavior, skill, etc. to another in such a way that the recipient of your amazing wisdom is then able to absorb that knowledge, change his behavior and teach that skill to someone else.

Therefore, I am not saying "to be understood" because I want the implication to be included in the word 'teach.' It is incumbent upon the teacher to first learn where his student is coming from. What is his or her current level of understanding, of knowledge. How does this student best learn? Is he a visual learner? Audio? Kinesthetic or perhaps something else? What state of mind is the student in? Is that state conducive to learning? If a student is so hungry that all he thinks about is food, good luck teaching him anything. I hope it was not a waste of time explaining that. I know I tend to go on and on. Please forgive me. Where were we?

So, let's begin the conversation differently. Let's watch what is going on for a couple minutes or maybe longer. Then let's approach with a smile and an extended hand. Maybe it could go something like this:

"Good morning, José. Buenos Días. Cómo estás? Did I say that right?"

"Buenos días, boss man. Yes, you said it right. Good Spanish."

"Ha, ha, ha. Thank you. So, I don't want to keep you from doing your work, but I must ask you something."

"Claro, sure, amigo. What is it?"

"Well, I have never seen that tool before, and I was wondering what it's called."

"Oh this? This is a cable puller. It grabs onto the wire or cable like this and then you attach a come along and you pull it through, so it does not slip."

"Oh, that's pretty slick."

"No boss. It's not slick at all because it has these teeth. See?"

"Ha, ha, ha. No, I mean it's pretty slick as in pretty cool. A great invention and I bet it reduces injuries to your hands and your back."

"Oh yes. It sure is and yes, I think it does. It makes it much more easier."

"José, there's something else I noticed that I need to ask you about. Where are your safety glasses?"

"Oh shoot! I left them in my truck at break. I'll go get them right now."

"Awesome. I usually see you with them on, so I wondered if something was wrong."

"Well, my wife she called me at break, and she was yelling because I left my socks on the floor again. Ha, ha, ha."

"Yeah, well, that can do it. Just remember to take some deep breaths whenever you feel frustrated. I know it always helps me. How are you feeling now?"

"Oh, I'm good, thanks, boss. I'll go grab those right now."

"Awesome! Thank you, José. I really enjoy working with you. You have a great attitude."

"Aww, thanks, boss. Do you need a hug? Ha, ha, ha."

"Ha, ha, ha. Jerk. No, but it's true. You can't imagine how many times I have to tell guys to put their safety glasses on and when I come back around the building, there they are with them in their pockets again. Guys like you make my job easier, and I just wanted to say thanks."

"Well, like you tell us, they are my eyes after all. I should be the one who cares the most about them."

"Exactly. Okay amigo, gracias y que tengas un buen día!"

"You too, amigo."

A conversation like this is quite typical on my jobsites. Let's break it down into steps.

- Compliment and/ or greet the worker as you approach.
- Recognize the safe behavior and express gratitude.
- Be professional in your criticisms. (Criticize the behavior not the worker)
- People have feelings and they tend to identify with their work (music, art, cooking, children, etc.)
- Insult their work and you insult their feelings, so be firm but gentle if possible.
- If possible, do not shame the worker in the front of his or her colleagues during the coaching session.
- Disrespecting the worker is the quickest way of losing the respect of such person.
- Demonstrate that you care about that worker by reminding him or her, "I want you to go home in the same or better condition that you arrived here today."

I realize that this took a few minutes, but did it make a difference do you think? Does José know that I care about him? Does he know that I appreciate his attitude about safety? Do you think he respects me and wants to do the right thing? Because that's what we are going for here. Correlating a positive feeling to a safe behavior. That is the power of SCIP. Sure, I could have just walked by and said nothing but then I wouldn't be doing my job. Or, I could have pointed at my glasses and told him to put his glasses on. Or I could have even used a little bit kinder approach and asked him where his glasses were, but none of those approaches compares to the Sandwich Approach. Try it. Use it often.

You can also use the safety incentive card to modify unsafe behaviors. Here is another example.

Example:

Safety Rick: Hey John, how's life in the fast lane?

John: Oh, hey Rick. Not bad. Just trying to get this project finished so we can move on to the next one.

Safety Rick: Yeah, I get it. Can I talk to you for just a second? I'll be quick. So, I wanted to give you a safety card for making sure that Gary's lanyard was properly attached to his harness. I just saw you do that, and I think that's very cool.

John: Oh yeah, we try to do that every time. You can't be too safe, you know. Gary just checked mine a minute ago. Can he get a card too?

Safety Rick: Yes, of course. Can I ask you something though?

John: Yeah, sure, what?

Safety Rick: What cut level gloves are required on site?

John: What do you mean?

Safety Rick: I mean, when you went through the safety orientation, you were told about the 100% glove policy. Do you remember what is the minimum cut level required? And, why you aren't wearing any gloves?

John: Oh shoot! I left them in my truck during break. And no, I don't remember about cut level.

(Awkward pause as John remains still, hoping Rick will give him a pass)

Safety Rick: Yeah, you need to always have them on while on site. Unless you are on break It is required.

John: Yes, I'll go grab those now. Thanks for the reminder, Rick. I honestly had them on earlier.

Safety Rick: Yes, I know. I saw you on my first round through. Thanks, John. You always have a good attitude about safety, and I appreciate that. Thank you. And cut level 3 is our minimum. If you're doing something that involves sharp materials or tools, you might need a cut level 5.

John: I remember you showed us the numbers on the backs of our gloves and the second one is the cut level. But yeah, man. It's about going home in one piece, right?

Safety Rick: Exactly. So, Gary, can I ask you a question?

Gary: Sure thing bro.

Safety person: You have your gloves on so, why did you not remind John to get his gloves? Do you remember our brother's keeper sticker? And what about 360 Degrees of Safety? I would have given you a brother's keeper hard hat sticker if you would have reminded him, and a safety card too. Maybe next time, yeah?

Gary: Cool, yeah bro. I'll try to watch for stuff like that.

Safety Rick: Awesome. It really takes all of us working together to make sure we all go home safely at the end of the day. Like I have said before, Dude! I can't be everywhere all the time, yeah? Ha, ha, ha.

Gary: Yeah, I have heard you say that before.

Safety Rick: Okay guys, well, thanks for your time. Please keep each other safe and have a great rest of your day.

Gary and John: Thanks Rick for watching out for us. It won't happen again.

Safety Rick: You guys, rock!

Why did I just give you two examples of basically the same thing? Because I can't stand it when I'm in some seminar or conference and the instructor is lecturing on the theory of this or that other thing and then the class is separated into groups where the instructor expects you to be able to perform. Therefore, I gave you two examples of what this Sandwich Approach could look like. Now you can practice. ☺

This is also a typical conversation. I have several of these each week.

Okay so, let's review what just happened here. I hope it's not pretentious of me to star in my own safety moment. Rick, the safety person, approached John who apparently had just entered a boom lift basket with Gary and was getting ready to ascend to do some patching on the building face. Rick rounded the corner in time to see John reach up and grab Gary's connecter and give it a tug. He was checking that Gary's lanyard connecter was properly attached to the "D" ring on the back of Gary's harness and located between Gary's shoulder blades. Rick approached in a friendly manner to break the ice and establish the tone of the conversation. John's response told Rick that John was in a bit of a hurry and did not want to waste much time chit-chatting. So, Rick cut to the chase and acknowledged John's safe behavior. But then Rick mentioned something else that he noticed and that was that John was not wearing any gloves. Gary was but John wasn't. Rick mentioned that fact and reminded John to keep them on. John made the decision to go get his gloves from his truck.

Another way to use a safety card as a motivator to modify unsafe behavior would be if, in this same scenario, Rick would have approached

Gary and given Gary a safety card for wearing the proper gloves. Then all Rick would have to do is look at John's ungloved hands and raise his eyebrows. John would undoubtedly get the message at which point John would say his gloves are in his truck. If John says nothing, then Rick would say, "John, where are yours?" and John would say, "Left 'em in the truck." Rick would say, "Well, I noticed you had them on earlier," and smile as John shrugs and went to get his gloves.

There are several ways the safety cards can be used as a reward and as an ice breaker to get the conversation to either safe or unsafe behaviors.

Using Names

I really can't impress enough how important this coaching technique is. My dad used to have a friend from the paper mill. We used to take our boats out on the Snake River on the weekends and we would go water skiing and pull huge inner tubes behind the boats. Then we'd come back in and there our moms would have a huge spread of picnic type foods under the gazebo on the concrete picnic table. There would be lawn darts set up or badminton and people who didn't like to ski or couldn't fit in the boat, because you can only haul so many people at one time, would be playing games or feeding their faces. The main thing I remember about Gene T. was that he never ever called anyone of us kids by our names. It's not like he didn't have the chance to learn them. I just don't think he wanted to badly enough to do it. He called everybody "Guy." Hey Guy, grab that ski and put it in the boat." "Hey Guy, would you bring me a beer since you're standing by the cooler?" "Hey Guy, this," and "hey Guy that." It's not very personal and after knowing him for over five years, you would think he would learn our names. I guess the moral of this story is, don't be like Gene. Learn your worker's names. It has been fifty years and I still know his first and last name.

If you travel to multiple jobsites, I can see how you might not recall everyone's name and that's okay. But don't be shy about saying, "I'm sorry, what was your name again? And don't think I'm not going to keep asking until I finally remember."

He could feel one of four ways about you not remembering his name. He might tease you and give you a hard time about it all in fun. He could get really butt-hurt over it, but I highly doubt that. He could not really give a black bilge rat's butt, however the most likely option is that he's going to appreciate the fact that you asked him his name and are making a point to use it. Then later that day if you are still on site, you can use his name again and he will appreciate that. When you use people's name it makes him or her feel valued. It gives them the sense that they matter to you. And they should matter to you. You wouldn't have a job without them.

'Seek first to understand, then to teach' is perhaps one of the most important aspects of this entire incentive program. Real teaching begins after the teacher finds out what the student's needs are, not before. Don't make the mistake of riding in on Power Trip, your great white horse, like you're going to save the day. Nobody appreciates that approach. Address him by name and ask him how he's doing. Ask him if he has any safety suggestions or concerns. Ask him why he is doing it like this exactly and if he thinks this is the safest way. Ask if he was trained on this piece of equipment or power tool and ask questions about that training. Ask if he has any documentation to verify training or if his company's office can provide that for you. After you have fully analyzed the situation, then ask him if he knows there is a better way, a safer way. Your approach may be the difference between this worker going home or going to the hospital. Trust me, you'll catch more bees with honey than vinegar.

Here are some other things to remember about using names.

- If workers use your name, that is them trying to be personable and show you respect. Reciprocate the favor.
- When you write their name on the safety card, always repeat their name out loud, and make sure you spell it correctly as a sign that you care enough to get their name right.
- Knowing you care, might encourage the worker to try to please you by complying with the safety policies, procedures, and standards.
- Using a worker's name makes it easier for him or her to accept any corrective criticisms you may give when using the Sandwich Approach.

To reiterate, always learn and use the worker's name prior to recognizing their safe behavior and before handing them their safety card. Write their name on the card. Write the behavior on the card. Write your name on the card or if another worker nominated someone for a safety card, then write the person who nominated the worker in place of your name.

Demonstrate you care about the worker. Look him or her in the eye and tell them you are proud of them. There is little that is more motivating than hearing someone whom you respect tell you that he is proud of you. I am reminded of the few times during my teenage years when my father would pull me aside to tell me how proud he was of me and the way I was living my life, of the good choices I was making, and I recall how that made me feel. It only inspired me to do better because I did not wish to disappoint him.

I wouldn't make this more complicated than it needs to be. If you carry a small notebook for notes, jot the names down in that. With writing things down there is a psycho-somatic brain body connection. We remember things better if we write them down. Otherwise, use the 'Notes' application on your phone and write who received a safety card and what it was for so you can acknowledge that person publicly the next morning. Don't forget to do this and if you start it, definitely don't forget anybody's name.

Private and Public Recognition

Not all societies are set up to use recognition as a reward, but the society in the West certainly is. In the entertainment industry we have Emmys and Grammys and Tonys and I don't know what all. In the media industry there are awards. In sports we give awards. In business there are awards and in school and just about every facet of life, we are recognized for accomplishments. It is what motivates many people to strive for excellence. It also gives bragging rights. So, not only did we receive the award, and we were recognized at the awards banquet, or wherever, but now we get to keep bringing it up in conversation to people we meet, on our resume or CV and on book bios. We seem to be all about recognition in our society.

I'm not saying it's a bad thing, necessarily. It is what it is. It does seem a little egocentric at times. But let's not fix it if it isn't broken. Rewards motivate people to be better, to achieve excellence and therefore we are going to capitalize on this basic human nature, the desire for attention.

It starts at a very young age, and I don't think it's something we are taught as much as we seek the approval of the people we love and respect. Later, it morphs into something less genuine than an innocent child hoping for the attention of his parents when he does a flip on the trampoline, but this basic need for attention and appreciation is what I have tried to incorporate into the SCIP system.

Don't freak out. It's fake. ;-)

Here are some tips to be aware of regarding public and private recognition.

- Recognize the workers in both public and private.
- This gesture helps build their confidence and enhances cooperation with the implementation of safety procedures in the organization.

- The recognized worker will feel more appreciated and work harder towards the realization of the company's safety goals.
- If you keep a log of all cards handed out on Monday, you can acknowledge those workers in the Tuesday safety huddle—say who got a card and what for.

Barriers to Coaching

Captain Smew, running from disgruntled workers.

I realize I have said this several times but seek to understand first, then seek to teach. If I don't feel like you care about me, why should I care about what you want to tell me? If you come in hot and heavy with your OSHA standard 1910-1926 yaddah yaddah, do you really think you are going to connect with me on a level that's going to do any good? Well, I can tell you. You aren't going to. What's going to happen is that you are going to scare me into compliance for as long as I think you are still on the project or lurking about and when I think that enough space and time has elapsed between you telling me to put my gloves on and now, then I'm going to take my gloves off. You didn't inspire me. You did not give me a reason why and the truth is, most people don't slow down for long enough to identify their own reason why so that's where our coaching comes in. We can share a touching safety moment with them. We can help them remember why they should hold their personal safety and health in such high regard. Do you have kids at home? Grandkids? A wife? A mother? Hobbies? Goals? These are all reasons why to not lose a finger, an eye, your hearing, or sustain a back injury. Do you want to be able to watch them grow up? Hear them laughing? Touch your wife? Make love to her? Be able to ride horses? Grow in the company? Be a solid income earner to support your family? Or would you rather be paralyzed, blind, crippled, unable to lift a gallon of milk, let alone your granddaughter? Trust me when I say, people do things for reasons. You just need to remind them of what those reasons are.

I have had two work-related back injuries and let me tell you they suck! The worse thing about a back injury, or shoulder injury, sciatica, or similar injuries is that nobody else can see them. That's right. Remember when we discussed wanting attention? It's no lie that women call us men babies when we get sick. It's because we want attention. We don't want it consciously. That would be being a wimp. That's not very manly or macho of us, but subconsciously, where our id lives, that is from whence this craving for attention stems. As much as you think you don't want or like attention, studies prove we die or go insane without it. Feeding this primal need is a continuation of the nurturing of our inner child if you will. I'm not referencing any of this for two reasons. I don't want to dig through my university psychology texts for one and it just seems like common knowledge to me.

But that's not the only issue with these types of injuries. You get judged. I mean, people whisper, and I can only imagine what they are saying. "Why is that jerk making his wife carry those groceries?" "Why doesn't he help her with those kids? What a POS!" "Why doesn't that lazy bum get a job?" "He doesn't look handicapped. Why is he parking in the handicapped spot when there are legit handicapped people who need that?" You can imagine. So yeah, that part really sucks.

Okay, I'll define 'id' for those who don't know. Webster *In Freudian theory, the division of the psyche that is totally unconscious and serves as the source of instinctual impulses and demands for immediate satisfaction of primitive needs.*

From Merriam-Webster.com it reads: *the one of the three divisions of the psyche in psychoanalytic theory that is completely unconscious and is the source of psychic energy derived from instinctual needs and drives.*

And here are some tips for this section on barriers.

- Overcome barriers during your coaching sessions.
- As a leader, the team is looking up for you to provide direction in case barriers are encountered during the coaching session.
- Be consistent in your coaching messaging to overcome most of the barriers.
- Seek first to understand, then seek to teach.
- As an observer, notice if the worker seems to be in a bad mood like these cannibals chasing Captain Smew!

CHAPTER 8

Incentives

Out-doggone-standing! We are almost to the end and now getting to the fun part. The incentives are the carrots we dangle in front of our workers. They are the little bit of leverage we can use to encourage the behavior we hope for. We know that unsafe behaviors lead to injuries, and we don't want any of those so only by replacing unsafe behaviors with safe behaviors can we achieve our goal of zero (or close to zero) injuries. Initially at least, let's shoot for injury reduction. That's a goal we can sink our teeth into. Do you agree?

Why do workers hold onto their cards? One reason is that safety cards aren't handed out like candy on Halloween. Not everyone gets one. That employee earned that exact card for something he or she did. It belongs to him/her, and it is his/her personal reward like a blue ribbon handed out to the first runner crossing the finish line of the 1000-meter run at a junior high school track meet. It's not hugely special but it is a little bit special.

Another reason to hold onto it is because the safety cards are tossed into a bucket at the weekly or monthly safety meeting where they become raffle tickets for a drawing.

The prizes do not need to be large because just winning anything is kind of fun for the workers. Depending on the group size, movie tickets or a gift certificate for dinner somewhere nice will suffice. I know for a fact that my daughter would love gift cards for a well known coffee chain. Be careful though. Some see gift cards as cash and taxable income. What else? Lunch coolers, Hitachi type bar-B-Q's make nice gifts. Heavy duty extension cords, tape measures, hammers, Klein electrician's tools, etc. Buy nice stuff. Don't cheap out but don't go high dollar either. That sounds contradictory. I mean buy nice quality tools but don't buy big ticket items like a Milwuakee™ Fuel Brushless hammer drill. The workers would love you for it, but those huge ticket items distract from the SCIP system's purpose, in my humble opinion. I almost always include candy bars and small boxes of candies to be able to have more winners. The workers like it, and it gets them more excited to be a part of the safety program. Never have I spent more than $200 in a month on prizes. You may choose to have enough apples, oranges, and bananas on hand too. Not for prizes but for anyone who wants one. I can assure you that gesture will go over well.

It is not necessary to go all out and make prizes the focal point of the safety program. The prizes are just the icing on the cake. Going home safely is the cake, the grand prize, and that message needs to be iterated often. The card itself is a reward. Guys take the cards home and show their families what they got today at work. It gives them another opportunity to reinforce the safe behavior via a teaching moment and it works like magic.

Raffle Prizes

If your raffle is held monthly, you might consider combining it with a safety meeting and offer donuts, electrolyte drinks, and fruit as snacks to all the workers in attendance. (They seem to really like bananas and apples and with more and more folks concerned about their health these days, it's a good idea to offer healthy options). This gesture also aids in garnering good attitudes. Incentives are given to reward safe behaviors that exceed the minimum job requirements. The gesture helps to garner good safety practice attitudes.

Ensure that there is a good sound system so that those in attendance can hear and understand the message being shared.

This Photo by Unknown Author is licensed under CC BY

The other reason to hold onto it is because the safety cards are tossed into a bucket at the monthly safety meeting where they become raffle tickets for a drawing. The prizes do not need to be large. Just winning something is kind of fun for the workers. You can get $20 - $50 tools at the hardware store of your choice. You could do some legwork and drum up donors for prizes that might include dinner for two at some swanky restaurant in town. We also draw for candy bars and small boxes of candies just to keep the cost down and to have more winners. Besides, who doesn't love a Snickers after stretch & flex?

Ensure you have a good sound system and that all the workers in the group, especially those in the rear, can hear and understand the message and the names being drawn. I usually lead them in Stretch & Flex, then have the safety meeting followed by the drawing.

Ideas for safety incentives:

- One reason employees hold onto their safety cards is because they earned them for something safety related that they did.
- Another reason is for Friday's raffle!!!
- Use prizes as incentives to reinforce safety in the workplace.
- The value of the prizes can be compared to being handed the first-place blue ribbon prize for winning a 1000m race in junior high.
- The memory is usually unforgettable.
- The prizes do not have to be big.
- Too large of prizes shift the program's focus away from safe behaviors and onto prizes.
- Day off passes
- Double time—Double worker's break time for an entire week.

- Breakfast with the boss/ 5-4 lunch
- An example could be a movie ticket or dinner for two.
- While the budget may allow for large power tools, big screen TVs, this tactic distracts from the program's objectives.
- Large prizes are reported to encourage cheating among workers.
- Prizes should not be the focal point of the safety program.
- The motivating driver for the safety team is to ensure that the workers reach their homes when they are safe.

"5-4 Lunch"

Another option for a drawing could be "5-4 lunch" where five names are drawn in the weekly raffle (or fewer if the overall crew size is small). Those lucky five get to have lunch with the GC management team and discuss topics ranging from anything to everything, except work. This '5-4-lunch' is all about getting to know your workers and letting them get to know you. As you build stronger relationships, workplace morale improves. When morale improves, good things tend to happen. One of those being an improved safety culture. When you walk the project and see one of the workers you just spent 30 minutes at lunch with, you will know a little something about him or her. Your genuine concern for that worker's well-being will be made apparent and when a worker knows you care about him, your message of safety has a much greater chance of making an impact.

- "5-4 lunch" is another incentive technique that you can use.
- Involves drawing five names in weekly raffles.
- Those lucky to be picked are granted the opportunity to have lunch with the General Contractor/ management team and allowed to discuss all topics on earth except work.
- This method is very effective at strengthening relationships.

This Photo by Unknown Author is licensed under CC BY

Challenge Coins

- One other cool idea I have tried, and seen others implement as incentives, are challenge coins. A challenge coin can be designed just about any way you want it to be. You can have an image, message, and/or project names on them. For colors they can be bronze, silver, gold or painted. I am not going to recommend any companies but if you do an online search for challenge coin manufacturers you won't come up empty handed. Challenge coins make great prizes and wonderful mementos.

r that you want

This Photo by Unknown Author is licensed under

- What is a challenge coin? To the uninitiated, challenge coins are just cool little trinkets. Paper weights. To prior service personnel, carrying a challenge coin means you don't have to buy the beer, or lunch. A challenge coin can be given to confirm membership in a special unit or group. It can convey a unique honor or commendation. It can be a heartfelt sign of appreciation.

- You could use challenge coins in other ways. "Good morning. Whoever does not have a challenge coin raise your hand?" Now pick one of these to lead Stretch & Flex or give the safety moment.

Brother's Keeper Sticker

Another incentive giveaway that I have done is a brother's keeper sticker for a toolbox, hard hat, or cell phone case. The sticker is one inch in diameter and has the image of a sequoia tree with the words, "Brother's Keeper" in the outer margin. The significance of using a sequoia tree, if you do not know, is that the roots of these trees are intertwined so that all the trees are linked together and act to hold one another up in a storm. Let that sink in a second. These stickers are given rarely on a project and only when a worker has gone above and beyond to help someone else out or to make the way safer for others. One key is that there needs to be initiative taken by the worker. His supervisor cannot have asked him to do the behavior. It must come from inside.

Brother's Keeper Sticker

- The sticker can be for toolboxes, hard hats, or cell phone cases
- The size can be 1" in diameter and contains an image of a sequoia tree
- The symbolism of using this species of tree is in linking the trees together through the intertwined roots to help them withstand the storm
- The brother's keeper sticker is given out to the most accomplished worker who went out of his way to help another worker to avert a safety disaster
- The incentive symbolizes the bravery that the worker demonstrated in making the way safer for others

This has nothing to do with the SCIP system, but it is something special or extra I do use the power of positive reinforcement to encourage the specific behavior of being a 'Brother's Keeper'. When I observe a worker go out of his or her way to bring coworkers a water or they remember to set up shade for everyone else when the temperature reaches 80 degrees, they make sure the egress/ exit is clear of debris and combustible materials, or anything like this; in fact, whenever their actions benefit one or more of their co-workers, that qualifies them to get noticed as a Brother's Keeper in my book. Two or three of these will get this sticker or a challenge coin. I don't hand very many of these out, not like safety cards. Hand it to the worker in the moment but remember to announce it in the morning huddle in front of everyone or even on Friday during the raffle.

Summary Points and Key Take-Aways

Every half-way decent lesson plan has an objective section as well as a summary.

Here are some of the things we covered here today. (Or as long as it took you to read this).

- OSHA declares that safety programs should only be tied to a safe behavior (not the absence of unsafe ones)
- The reason for workplace safety is to prevent injuries at work.
- Seek first to understand, then seek to teach.
- Safety culture can be improved through positive reinforcement.
- SCIP is a type of tool in a behavior-based safety program toolbox.
- Behaviors can be safe or unsafe.

- Safe behaviors can be reinforced using safety incentive cards.
- The key to injury reduction is to replace unsafe behaviors with safe ones.
- What were some of your key take-aways?
- What are you going to do differently?
- What are you going to do more of?
- How can SCIP improve the safety culture in your workplace?

QUESTIONS?

Avast me hearties!

Me dear ol' mum, bless 'er black soul, tol me to ask if ye scurvy sea dogs 'ave any riddles wot ye been ponderin', an' if it be so, ye best be fer askin', savvy? Now I'll be swillin' a pint or two o' grog an' 'ave a bit of a lie down, if ye don't mind.

And that means, do you have any questions?

OSHA verification

A comment I sometimes respond to:

Remember when someone tells you that OSHA no longer allows safety incentive programs (oddly enough, more than five years after this 2018 letter, people are still telling me that, "you can't have a safety incentive program") you can tell them that's not an accurate statement.

In an October 11, 2018, OSHA letter of interpretation regarding https://www.osha.gov/laws-regs/interlinking/stand-ards/1904.35(b)(1)(iv) the clarification was made to an earlier final rule dated May 16th, 2016, which amended a standard by adding the provision that OSHA prohibits *"employers from retaliating against employees for reporting work-related injuries or illnesses."* Not receiving a reward or incentive was taken as retaliation for having reported an injury so it was commonly understood that incentive programs would have to be stopped. Lucky for me, I was ahead of my time. In fact, over two years before the initial ruling in 2016, I had been focusing on rewarding leading not lagging indicators. A safe behavior is a leading indicator while an injury is a lagging indicator.

As mentioned previously, most safety incentive programs used to reward workers for so many "safe days" without an injury or without a lost time injury/ illness. As this practice tends to discourage workers from reporting injuries, these types of "safety incentive" programs were disallowed. However, enough people needed further explanation, apparently, hence the need for this letter (https://www.osha.gov/laws-regs/standardinterpretations/2018-10-11) which allows the rewarding of the following activities, which were listed as acceptable by OSHA.

- *an incentive program that rewards employees for identifying unsafe conditions in the workplace.*
- *a training program for all employees to reinforce reporting rights and responsibilities and emphasizes the employer's non-retaliation policy.*
- *a mechanism for accurately evaluating employees' willingness to report injuries and illnesses.*
- *rewards workers for reporting near-misses or hazards and encourages involvement in a safety and health management system.*

As the Safety Card Incentive Program incentivizes and encourages *"participation in a safety and health management system"*, and encourages the reporting of leading indicators, stopping near misses, encouraging and reporting of safe behaviors, reporting unsafe conditions, etc., and is clearly designed *"to promote workplace safety and health,"* *"and would demonstrate that the employer is serious about creating a culture of safety,"* it does not appear to violate any aspect of OSHA's position on workplace safety incentive programs, or more specifically, 29 C.F.R. § 1904.35.

ASSESSMENT QUESTIONS

1. Explain what you understand by the term reinforcement and the categories involved

2. Why would you recommend a BBS Program as a Safety Technique?

3. A worker has committed an offence that you consider to be Unsafe 3 Behavior. Why do you think such employee should not be allowed to continue working on that day?

4. Safety cards are resourceful tools in safety incentive programs. List two reasons why.

5. Why is the Sandwich approach instrumental in coaching safety skills?

6. Seek first to _____, then _____ to _____.

7. Name 3 Safety Card Incentive Program benefits.

8. Name 3 SCIP incentives.

9. When should you use a worker's name in relation to when you hand them the card?

10. What goes inside the Sandwich Approach?

Assessment Answers

1. Ans: Operant conditioning refers to actions that enhance the chance of a desired response to occur.
2. Ans: Helps organizations to minimize compensation costs.
3. Ans: The offense is not caused by momentary lapse and has a potential of causing serious injuries or even death. Maintaining the worker at the site poses a risk.
4. Ans: Used to reinforce safety behavior and teach new skills.
5. Ans: Ensures that you give workers something to feel good about and a moment to reflect on unsafe behaviors.
6. Ans: Seek first to understand, then seek to teach.
7. Ans: a. Improves safety culture b. Improves worker morale c. Reduces injuries d. Reduces costs e. Makes safety fun f. all the above
8. Ans: Too many to list.
9. Ans: a. Before b. After c. During d. Just call them "Guy"
10. Ans: a. Using their name b. Ham and eggs c. Bacon, lettuce, and tomato d. Constructive criticism.

EPILOGUE/CONCLUSION

By implementing the Safety Card Incentive Program, you can turn your waning safety culture around and make safety meaningful and fun. Watch as your morale on the jobsite improves. Watch as workers ask their foreman, "Was that lift good enough for a safety card?" and similar questions. Your recordable injuries should be reduced. Your overall injuries will likely be reduced. Several times a day workers will come to you with unsafe situations they have observed or unsafe situations they have rectified. As injury rates drop, so will your insurance claims and eventually so too will your worker's compensation premiums, unless you are self-insured, obviously. Then you'll just be paying out less.

It doesn't have to cost a lot of money, and it shouldn't. If you raffle off high dollar prizes, you'll distract from the main objective of this program which is to bring safety top of mind for your workers. Instead of safety as a primary focus, it will be that trip to Hawaii you are raffling off on Friday. Resist the temptation is my advice. Take that for what it's worth.

So, design and order your cards and train your team on this method using positive reinforcement to encourage safe behaviors in your workplace. I wish you the best of success as you strive toward a goal of zero injuries, so everybody can go home in the same, or better, condition that they arrived.

BIBLIOGRAPHY

Learning Resources

- https://www.merriam-webster.com/dictionary/learning
- https://allpsych.com/psychology101/reinforcement/
- https://allpsych.com/psychology101/reinforcement/
- https://www.youtube.com/watch?v=JA96Fba-WHk

Ramlall, S. J., Al-Kahtani, A., & Damanhouri, H. (2014). Positive organizational Behavior in the workplace: A cross-cultural perspective. International Journal of Management & Information Systems (IJMIS), 18(3), 149-154.

Itri, J. N., Bruno, M. A., Lalwani, N., Munden, R. F., & Tappouni, R. (2019). The incentive dilemma: Intrinsic motivation and workplace performance. Journal of the American College of Radiology, 16(1), 39-44.

Stagg, S. J., Sheridan, D. J., Jones, R. A., & Speroni, K. G. (2013). Workplace bullying: The effectiveness of a workplace program. Workplace Health & Safety, 61(8), 333-338.

Hofmann, D. A., Burke, M. J., & Zohar, D. (2017). 100 years of occupational safety research: From basic protections and work analysis to a multilevel view of workplace safety and risk. Journal of applied psychology, 102(3), 375.

Kisner, T. (2018). Workplace incivility: How do you address it? Nursing2020, 48(6), 36-40.

Verma, A., Gupta, A., & Nangia, G. (2014). Study of Various Adaptation Policies by Companies to Compete at a Global Scenario. Global Journal of Finance and Management, 6(7), 615-618.

Zhang, M., & Fang, D. (2013). A continuous behavior-based safety strategy for persistent safety improvement in construction industry. Automation in Construction, 34, 101-107.

Wang, X., Xing, Y., Luo, L., & Yu, R. (2018). Evaluating the effectiveness of Behavior-Based Safety education methods for commercial vehicle drivers. Accident Analysis & Prevention, 117, 114-120.

UVEX Bionic Face Shield (S8500) — (https://www.amazon.com/dp/B001VXXUWK/_encoding=UTF8?coliid=I3VJGEIREYMKH7&colid=6CACM77KAKVL&psc=1&redirectFromSmile=1).

ACKNOWLEDGEMENTS

Last night I was telling my special lady friend about the 'acknowledgements section' of my book, which was one of the last things on my "to-do list." I jokingly said that I should thank myself for creating the cover, writing the body, doing the first few edits, writing the book blurb, conducting the SEO research, not giving up, and even for the future marketing and website creation. The truth is that I did everything myself, and while I'm not sure if that's a good thing, it's my creation and I'm proud of it.

On a more serious note, I would like to express my gratitude to a few people who inspire me to be better, to achieve more, and to reach higher. Any list of people I am grateful for must start with my loving Father in Heaven. Without the divine gifts of curiosity, intelligence, and determination that I have been blessed with, this project would have failed long ago.

In the non-supernatural realm, I have a good friend and colleague, Heather Densley, who has encouraged me throughout my journey of becoming a certified safety professional (ASP then CSP-I'll take the CSP test soon, Heather!) and in completing this book project. We affectionately refer to Heather as "Mom" because of her vast knowledge and unwavering support. I want to extend a heartfelt thank you to Heather.

I would be remiss if I didn't mention my good friend, colleague and 'boss-man (he dislikes us calling him that),' Trevor Austin. He gives me the freedom to do my work and always lets me know that he believes in me and is there for me if I need him. I have learned so much from his management style and am forever grateful for his support.

Also, I want to thank my daughter Chelsea and her husband, Alex Laird for their constant encouragement and support. They must often wonder why I spend so many hours holed up in my room studying, writing, researching, reading, and working. (Yesterday I worked from 7 a.m. to 2 a.m.). Typical. I am eternally grateful to them for giving me the daily doses of love that only family can give.

My son Rick calls and texts me frequently, just to talk and to stay close, even though we are 857 miles apart. I love that he shares his construction work with me and often I even understand what he's talking about. He is an electrician in the Nampa, Idaho area and very good at what he does. (Shameless plug). I miss you, son.

Lastly, but certainly not least, I want to acknowledge my special lady friend, Gwen Yeung. She understands me like nobody else, except possibly my mother. If there were a female Chinese version of myself, that person would perceive the world in similar fashion. Gwen, I am grateful for your unwavering support and your generous encouragement. Last night, I thanked her and told her that "a good woman can either make or break a man and a strong man becomes even stronger with a good woman supporting him." Her humble response was "Yes, I know." Positive reinforcement is a powerful tool when used correctly. Thank you dear for understanding and giving me free rein to pursue my dreams.

ABOUT THE AUTHOR

As of the writing of this book, Richard Wayne Dyer lives in San Jacinto, California and works as an Environmental Safety & Health Manager for Layton Construction LLC, based in Irvine, CA. He holds an OSHA 500, OSHA 501, ASP, OHST, CHST, EM383-1-1, HAZWOPER 40, and several other certifications and courses. His decision to pursue a career in safety was influenced by his experiences working in the military, emergency medical, healthcare, construction, and general industries, as well as earning a Bachelor of Science degree in Occupational health & Safety from Columbia Southern University. After two work related neck & back injuries, he decided to find a career that did not involve such physically demanding work and became a full-time safety professional. Now he gets to use his brains and his heart. He oversees multi-million-dollar construction projects and works with ESH managers in Nevada, Washington, and California for Layton Construction Company, LLC. He worked and lived for 15 years in Hawaii prior to hiring on at Layton in May of 2019.

Dyer is also the creator of the "Safety Card Incentive Program," which he developed while working for the non-profit Partners in Development Foundation in Hawaii. Through this program, he was able to reduce recordable injuries from 29 in 2013 to just 3 in each of his last two years there. Their website is: https://pidf.org and the author encourages you to investigate all the good they bring to the Ohana of Hawaii.

Dyer is also the author of a tween book series called, *Seven Deadly Sins of a Pirate*. So far only *Smew's Greed Parts I & II* are published on Amazon.com as of the writing of this non-fiction in February of 2023. Rest assured; others are forthcoming.

THE END

Made in the USA
Columbia, SC
08 February 2025

53500854R00078